IMAGES
of Sport

SOMERSET COUNTY CRICKET CLUB

Two giants of Somerset cricket: Viv Richards and Ian Botham.

IMAGES
of Sport

SOMERSET COUNTY CRICKET CLUB

Compiled from
The Archives of Somerset Cricket Museum

TEMPUS

First published 1999
Copyright © Somerset Cricket Museum, 1999

Tempus Publishing Limited
The Mill, Brimscombe Port,
Stroud, Gloucestershire, GL5 2QG

ISBN 0 7524 1585 9

Typesetting and origination by
Tempus Publishing Limited
Printed in Great Britain by
Midway Clark Printing, Wiltshire

Some other sports titles from Tempus Publishing:

Bristol Rovers FC
Glamorgan CCC
Glamorgan CCC the Second Selection
Exeter City FC
The FA Cup Final Between the Wars
Plymouth Argyle FC 1886-1986
The Scarborough Festival
Surrey CCC
Torquay United FC
Yorkshire CCC

This postcard of the county ground at Taunton dates from 1904.

Contents

Acknowledgements

The illustrations in this book, with only a few exceptions, are from the archive of Somerset Cricket Museum at Taunton. Thanks to Eddie Lawrence and to Barry Knott, sports editor at the *Somerset County Gazette*, for helping to fill one or two gaps.

The museum's collection of many hundreds of photographs and other illustrations has been long in the making. Newspapers and individual photographers have been generous in providing copies over the years and, among the latter group, Alain Lockyer deserves a special mention. Many members of the cricket club have donated photographs and other archive material and, of course, such donations – as well as gifts or the loan of other cricket memorabilia – are always most welcome.

The many books consulted for this project include Peter Roebuck's *From Sammy to Jimmy* (1991) and David Foot's *Sunshine, Sixes and Cider* (1986), both of which have been invaluable, while Nigel Johns' *Somerset CCC First-class Records 1882-1995* has been indispensable for statistics.

Finally, a grateful thanks to Clifford Jiggens, without whose hard work and dedication this book would not have been possible.

The museum is a registered charity and all of its proceeds from the sale of this book will be devoted to further improving and extending the display of exhibits.

Introduction

The earliest recorded cricket in Somerset was at Bath in 1751, although the game was doubtless played in the county in some fashion in earlier decades. It was nearly seventy years later that the first club was formed (again at Bath), and then in the 1820s and 1830s more clubs sprang up across the county, including one at Taunton.

In August 1875, the Gentlemen of Somerset, who had been playing fairly regularly for the previous fifteen years, visited Sidmouth, where they met and defeated the Gentlemen of Devon. Before leaving the Devon seaside town, the victors held a meeting at which it was decided to found a County Cricket Club for Somerset.

The intention was not to have a county ground, and for several years this was so. Matches were played at venues around the county – those held at Taunton took place at Fullands School, which boasted one of the best grounds in the West Country.

However, in 1881 Taunton Athletic Club, representing various sporting interests, including cricket, opened a sports centre on the old Priory Fields beside the River Tone, and very soon this was to become the home of Somerset cricket.

Somerset played there for the first time in 1882, their matches that year including the first visit by the Australian tourists. Fixtures were mainly against other counties and twenty-seven matches on the ground in the first four years have retrospectively been given first-class status.

But things were not going too well for Somerset, either on or off the field (a situation which has repeated itself several times over the past century). Fortunately, there was a man on hand to deal with things: this man was Henry Murray-Anderdon. He took over as honorary secretary at a critical moment and stayed in the job for twenty-five years. He soon claimed the ground for Somerset, secured a lease and before the end of the century the club had purchased it. The county owes him a great debt.

Two other men were on the scene to truly put Somerset on the first-class cricket map. First there was Herbert Hewett – sometimes called 'The Colonel' – a forthright, stubborn character who was not only a forceful leader but a fine left-handed batsman. He once shared an opening stand of 346 with Lionel Palairet (which still stands as a Somerset record for any wicket). The second was Sammy Woods, a rumbustious Australian who was a fiery bowler, aggressive batsman and one of cricket's greatest 'characters'. In 1890, Hewlett led Somerset, who were still looked upon as a second-rate county, to an incredibly successful season, and the following year there could be no denying them a place in the new first-class county championship. Somerset had arrived!

Hewlett quit after three years in the Championship, feeling aggrieved over the way the club had handled a match against the Australians, and Woods took over. Thirteen years later, when he gave up the captaincy, Wisden observed that more than anyone else Woods had been the 'making of Somerset cricket'.

For several decades, Somerset teams were largely made up of amateurs – some of them talented cricketers, others there to make up the numbers. Somerset relied on amateurs longer and to a greater extent than any other county.

Somerset have never won the Championship (they have been third on four occasions), and had not won any title until 1979, when they took the Gillette Cup and were also Sunday League champions. However, Somerset cricket has always been entertaining and the side full of characters and so they are popular on any ground.

The photographs that appear in this book, almost all of them having been taken from the museum's archives, have been chosen to give something of the flavour of Somerset cricket. The triumphs and the great players are here, of course, but so are many of the ordinary ones who provide the backbone of a team. There are also some lesser amateurs of particular interest and others who, although they have never played for Somerset, have contributed much to the club's story and have been familiar faces around the ground. A number of much-published pictures have been omitted to make room for lesser-known ones, some of which appear in this book for the first time.

Tony Stedall
Curator

One

Early Years

For its first half century or so, Somerset was largely an amateur side. Up until the First World War there were usually two or three professionals, needed especially to do the hard work of bowling, but for the rest it was men from the Universities, public schools, the Church, the legal profession, the Army and the Navy – not to mention the gentlemen of 'independent means' – who made up the eleven. These players were not always available when required and sometimes the captain (an amateur of course) had a job in getting together a full team.

A few of the amateurs were good enough to play international cricket – like Lionel Palairet and Sammy Woods – but many of the rest were really only club cricketers. The professionals of this period were headed by Ted Tyler, George Nichols, Ernie Robson and one of Somerset's greatest all-rounders, Len Braund.

Never serious contenders for the championship title, Somerset became 'The team of surprises' through their ability to beat the champion counties, notably Yorkshire, who lost only two matches in three triumphant years – both to the lowly West Country men.

SOMERSET COUNTY CRICKET MATCHES.—At a meeting of the Somerset Eleven, held at Sidmouth on Wednesday, 18th August, after the Somerset and Devon county match, the Rev. A. C. Ainslie in the chair, it was resolved— (1)—That it is desirable to organise annual matches against the neighbouring counties, and against first-class clubs, such as the Incogniti, &c. (2)—That the secretaries of leading cricket clubs in Somerset be communicated with on the subject, and their co-operation be invited. (3)— That the clubs which possess first-rate grounds in convenient situations be requested to allow the use of their grounds for the county matches; and, lastly, proposed by the Chairman, and seconded by the Rev. S. C. Voules, that Mr. Edward Western, of Fullands, Taunton, be requested to act as county secretary.

The birth of Somerset County Cricket Club in 1875, as reported in the *Somerset County Gazette.*

The county ground almost a century ago.

The Australian cricketers visited Somerset for the first time on 21 and 22 August 1882, during their third tour of this country. The match – which was one of the first to be played on the county ground – resulted in an innings win for the tourists, who scored 245 and dismissed Somerset for 96 and 130. The Australian captain and star batsman (and frequently wicketkeeper too) Billy Murdoch is in the forefront wearing pads and next to him is the famous stonewaller, A.C. Bannerman. Behind, from left to right, are: S.P. Jones, H.F. Boyle, T. Horan, G.J. Bonnor, C.W. Beal (*tour manager*), H.H. Massie and J. Blackham. One of those who missed this Victorian photocall was Fred Spofforth, the great fast bowler known as 'The Demon', who was Man of the Match. In Somerset's first innings he took all but the last wicket, with 9 for 51, and he took four in the second innings.

THE SECOND-CLASS
COUNTY CHAMPIONSHIP,
◁▷ 1890 ◁▷

COUNTY.	Somersetshire.	Derbyshire.	Cheshire.	Hampshire.	Leicestershire.	Warwickshire.	Essex.	Staffordshire.	Matches Play'd	Won.	Lost.	Drawn.	Points.
Somersetshire	...	...	...	WW	WW	WW	...	WW	8	8	0	0	8—
Derbyshire ...	...	...	...	...	WW	...	WL	...	4	3	1	0	2—
Cheshire ..	...	...	...	...	...	DD	...	DW	4	1	0	3	1—
Hampshire ...	LL	...	...	...	...	...	...	WW	4	2	2	0	0—
Leicestershire	LL	LL	...	...	..	LW	WW	...	8	3	5	0	—2
Warwickshire	LL	..	DD	...	WL	...	DD	..	8	1	3	4	—2
Essex ...	...	LW	...	...	LL	DD	...	...	6	1	3	2	—2
Staffordshire	LL	...	DL	LL	...	...	...	...	6	0	5	1	—2

Somerset were the undisputed top team among the second-class counties in 1890, and next season entered the first-class championship.

Herbert Hewett, known as 'The Colonel', captained Somerset in the early 1890s. A barrister, he was one of the best left-handed batsmen of his day and contributed 201 to the 346 first-wicket partnership with Lionel Palairet against Yorkshire in 1892 (see page 21).

Somerset cricketers, 1891. From left to right, back row: E.J. Tyler, G. Fowler, A.P. Wickham, R.C.N. Palairet, J.B. Challen. Middle row: S.M.J. Woods, L.C.H. Palairet, V.T. Hill, C.J. Robinson. Front row: H. Murray-Anderdon (*club secretary*), W.N. Roe, H.T. Hewett (*captain*), A.E. Newton, and G.B. Nichols (the lattermost pair being the club's two professionals).

Sir Spencer Ponsonby-Fane was president of the Somerset club for a quarter of a century until his death at the family's country seat at Brympton, near Yeovil, in 1915, aged ninety-one. Besides his leadership at Somerset, he held responsible offices at Court and the Foreign Office and, for thirty-five years, was treasurer of the MCC – for whom he played the first of many matches when only fifteen years old. He was a founder of I Zingari, the world's oldest surviving touring club. Last, and not least amongst his achievements, Sir Spencer built up the great art collection that is one of the treasures of Lord's.

Somerset cricket owes a tremendous debt to Henry Murray-Anderdon, who was associated with the club for forty years. He took over as honorary secretary at a critical time, held the office for a quarter of a century, and was president for several years until his death in 1922. He was also a member of the MCC Advisory Committee.

A Somerset XI of 1895. From left to right: W.C. Hedley, L.C.H. Palairet, M.N. Roe, C.E. Dunlop, A.E. Newton, S.M.J. Woods (*captain*), G.B. Nichols, E.J. Tyler, V.T. Hill, R.C.N. Palairet, G. Fowler. Nichols and Tyler were the only professionals.

Australian-born Sammy Woods took over from Hewett in 1894, and was captain for thirteen seasons, during which Somerset were firmly established on the first-class cricket map. In his younger days a fiery bowler, who once took all ten wickets, Woods became an aggressive batsman, whose double century in 135 minutes was the fastest in Victorian times and remains the fastest by a Somerset player to this day. An inspiring captain, he abhorred drawn games. He played test cricket for both England and Australia, and captained the Gentlemen.

Sammy, who adopted Somerset as his home, played rugby for England – several times as captain. He enjoyed almost every sport, but cricket was his first love. This picture, from the late 1920s, is probably the last of him as a cricketer. It was taken at the village of Broadway, in south Somerset.

Sammy Woods was a great favourite with the cartoonists. He was not only an all-round sportsman, but a great character as well. Were he around today, his exploits on and off the field would have ensured frequent appearances in the tabloids. Many cartoons, such as this one by 'Rip', refer to the White Rose county or its captain, Lord Hawke. Lowly Somerset inflicted some remarkable defeats around a century ago on Yorkshire, then one of the champion counties, and Woods' men earned the title of 'The team of surprises'. The most incredible match was that of 1901.

Yorkshire v. Somerset,

At Headingley, Leeds, July 15, 16, and 17, 1901.

Umpires :—Messrs. W. Wright & T. Mycroft.   Draw at 6-30

SOMERSET.

1	L. C. H. Palairet	b Hirst :	0	c & b Brown ...	173
2	Braund	b Rhodes... ...	0	b Haigh ...	107
3	Lewis	c Tunnicliffe b Rhodes	10	b Rhodes ...	12
4	F. A. Phillips	b Hirst	12	b Wainwright ...	122
5	S. M. J. Woods	c Hunter b Haigh	46	c Tunnicliffe b Hirst	66
6	V. T. Hill	run out	0	c Hirst b Rhodes	53
7	Robson	c Hunter b Rhodes	0	c Tunnicliffe b Rhodes	40
8	Gill ...	c Hunter b Rhodes	4	stp. Hunter b Rhodes	14
9	A. E. Newton	b Haigh	0	c Taylor b Rhodes	4
10	G. Burrington	c Brown b Rhodes	11	stp. Hunter b Rhodes	15
11	Cranfield	not out ...	1	not out ...	5
		Extras	3	Extras	19
		Total	87	Total	630

Total Runs at the fall of each wicket.

0 0 16 32 38 38 64 65 86 | 222 244 341 466 522 570 597 604 609

Bowling.	Overs.	Maidens.	Runs.	Wickets.	Overs.	Maidens.	Runs.	Wickets
Hirst ...	12	5	36	2	37	1	189	1
Rhodes ...	16	8	39	5	46.5	12	145	6
Haigh ...	4	0	9	2	20	4	78	1
Wainwright	...	...	...	...	34	3	107	1
Brown ...					18		92	1

Hirst, 3 n balls

NEW INN, Best Refreshments, Largest and Best Rooms in Headingley.

YORKSHIRE.

1	Brown	c Braund b Cranfield	24	c Sub b Gill ...	5
2	Tunnicliffe	c Newton b Gill ...	9	c Palairet b Braund	44
3	Denton	c Woods b Gill ...	12	b Braund ...	16
4	T. L. Taylor	b Cranfield ...	1	retired, hurt ...	0
5	F. Mitchell	b Gill ...	4	b Braund ...	21
6	Hirst	c Robson b Cranfield	61	lbw b Braund ..	6
7	Wainwright	b Gill	9	c Lewis b Cranfield	1
8	Lord Hawke	b Robson ...	37	c Burrington b Cranfield	4
9	Haigh	c Robson b Cranfield	96	not out ...	2
10	Rhodes	c Lewis b Robson ...	44	stp Newton b Cranfield	0
11	Hunter	not out	10	c Woods b Cranfield	0
		Extras	18	Extras	14
		Total	325	Total	113

Total Runs at the fall of each wicket.

13 33 44 51 55 86 142 167 285 14 57 91 99 104 109 109 109

Bowling.	Overs.	Maidens.	Runs.	Wickets.	Overs.	Maidens.	Runs.	Wickets
Cranfield	27	5	113	4 5 w's	18	5	35	4
Gill ...	23	2	105	4	4	1	23	1
Braund ...	5	0	33	0	15	3	41	4
Robson ...	10	1	35	2	...	...	...	...
Woods ...	5	1	21	0				
Palairet ...	1	1	0	0				

The team which beat Yorkshire in 1901. From left to right, back row: G.C. Gill, E. Robson, L. Braund, G. Burrington. Middle row: F.A. Phillips, A.E. Newton, S.M.J. Woods, L.C.H. Palairet, V.T. Hill. Front row: L.L. Cranfield, A.E. Lewis.

Vernon Hill, a left-handed batsman, put on 240 for the seventh wicket with Sammy Woods against Kent at Taunton in 1898, a record which stood until 1996. Hill played 121 times for Somerset. His brother, Eustace, had a couple of matches, and Vernon's sons, Evelyn and Mervyn, added over 50 county games to the family total. Vernon Hill was Somerset's president in 1930.

No matter how warm the day, Palairet is certain to have a handkerchief round his neck.

Wisden said of the tall, graceful opening batsman Lionel Palairet, 'Among the players of his day, there is no better to look at'. His shots, a later writer said, were 'All works of art', and his timing was superb. He hit twenty-seven centuries for Somerset, his best score being 292, and he averaged nearly 36 in over 400 innings in Somerset's first two decades in the championship. However, he only played in two Tests. In 1929 he was Somerset's president.

Richard Palairet, a year younger than Lionel, played fairly regularly for Somerset and might have rivalled his brother had he not damaged a knee playing soccer. He later became an administrator, becoming Surrey's secretary for thirteen years and joint manager of the MCC team during the 1932/33 'Bodyline' tour of Australia. He was Somerset's president from 1937 until 1946.

Lionel Palairet (132) and Herbert Hewett (201) scored 346 for the first wicket against Yorkshire at Taunton in 1892. It is still Somerset's best partnership for any wicket.

Gerald Fowler, the youngest of three cricketing brothers, opened the batting with Hewett in Somerset's first championship match and was also a fast-medium bowler. He served Somerset as treasurer for twenty years, and was secretary for a year or two. His brother, William, remembered as being a big hitter, also played for Somerset and all three (the other brother was called Howard) played for Oxford University.

Arthur Newton really disliked standing back, even to fast bowlers, and 119 of his 296 wicketkeeping victims for Somerset were stumped. His career with the county began in its second-class days and spanned thirty-five years. He turned out for Somerset Stragglers at the age of seventy-five and, six years later, was still playing club cricket! He had two tours: to North America and to Australia.

A Somerset trio in those days when wicketkeepers stood up to the fast men. Between them, from the late Victorian period up until the First World War, Henry Martyn, the Revd Archdale Wickham and Arthur Newton claimed 659 victims – of whom 202 were stumped. All three players were Oxford Blues. Martyn was also a useful bat, once hitting 1,000 runs in a season and scoring an unbeaten century against the Australians.

Cricketing metaphors featured in the sermons of the Revd Archdale Wickham, who became a Prebendary of Wells Cathedral. Over half (48) of his 83 victims as a Somerset wicketkeeper were stumped. When Hampshire scored 627-7 off the county, 'The Bishop' (as he was sometimes called) did not concede one bye.

SOMERSET COUNTY CRICKET CLUB.

BALANCE SHEET TO NOVEMBER 10th, 1899.

CAPITAL ACCOUNT.

	£ s. d.		£ s. d.
To Purchase of Ground, &c.	2850 0 0	By 114 Debentures @ £25 each	2850 0 0

CURRENT ACCOUNT.

	£ s. d.	£ s. d.		£ s. d.	£ s. d.
To Balance in favour of Club, Nov. 8, 1898		0 15 5	By Professional Expenses :—		
,, Members' Subscriptions ...		964 8 0	County Matches	469 18 6	
,, Subscriptions from the following Clubs:—			Ground Bowlers	393 15 9	863 14 3
Castle Cary C.C.	1 1 0		,, Tyler's Benefit (Gate) ...	69 6 0	
Taunton C.C.	1 1 0		,, Do. do. (Donation from Club)	10 10 0	79 16 0
Lansdowne C.C.	1 1 0				
Wells Athletic Union ...	2 0 0		,, Amateurs' Match and Hotel Expenses		269 11 11
Yeovil C.C.	1 1 0		,, Luncheons and Teas for Teams		153 14 5
Chard C.C.	1 1 0		,, Umpires		111 0 0
Bridgwater C.C.	1 1 0	8 6 0	,, Scorer		66 10 0
,, Gate Receipts at Matches :—			,, Ground Expenses :—		
Trial Match	3 15 6		Ground Men's Wages, &c. ...	184 18 6	
Lancashire	85 19 3		Gatekeepers	25 5 0	
Yorkshire	43 7 0		Pavilion Attendant ...	2 17 6	
Kent	28 6 6		Cleaning Grand Stands, Pavilion, Lavatories & Sundries	22 18 5	
Hants	77 11 6		New Mowing Machine ...	16 16 0	
Middlesex	139 2 6		Hire of extra Stand ...	25 0 0	
Sussex	190 17 0		Hire of Chairs ...	8 5 2	
Surrey	103 18 3		Gravel and Tar	6 19 6	
Australians	664 15 6		Grass Seed	2 11 0	
Gloucester	55 1 0	1392 14 0	Police Services	1 16 5	
,, Hire of Ground :—			Rates, Taxes and Water ...	35 17 6	
Doctors and Lawyers ..	1 1 0		Keep of Horse	22 2 0	
Tennis Club ...	5 0 0		Shoeing do.	0 15 0	
Town Council and Market Trustees	1 1 0		Mettam, Expenses at Bath ...	8 5 0	
Taunton Cricket Club ...	20 0 0		New Chairs, &c.	25 8 6	
Taunton Harriers	5 0 0		Sundry Repairs & Alterations, &c.	43 18 10	433 14 4
Hockey Club	5 0 0				
Private...	7 5 0	44 7 0	,, Printing Annual Cricket Books, General Printing, Advertising, &c.	76 12 11	
,, Professionals' Services ...		10 0 0	Bill Posting	12 14 0	
,, Refreshment Contract ...		55 0 0	Compiling Cricket Annual ...	5 5 0	
,, Sale of " Score " Cards ...		20 0 0	Postage	3 5 5	97 17 4
,, Advertisements in Cricket Book, &c.		11 0 0	,, Secretary's Salary... ...		200 0 0
,, Share of " Test " Matches ...		180 0 0	,, Accountant's Fee	7 7 0	
,, Sundries		6 9 6	Insurance	4 5 7	
			,, (Australian Match) ..	23 15 4	
			Cricket Material	31 11 0	
			Bank Charges & Cheque Books	3 13 3	
			Sundries	10 17 11	81 10 1
			,, Debenture Interest ...		110 4 0
			,, Australians (Share of Gate) ...		221 16 0
			,, Balance in favour of Club ...		3 11 7
		£2692 19 11			£2692 19 11

GERALD FOWLER, Treasurer.

Audited and found correct, December 11th, 1899,

ALEX. HAMMETT.

Where the money went in 1899 – including £22 for keep of the horse.

Jack MacBryan, whose Somerset career was from 1911 until 1931, topped the county's batting average several times, and he notched a total of eighteen centuries. Called up to play the South Africans in 1924, his only Test match was soon ruined by rain and he did not bat. MacBryan spent almost all the war in prisoner of war camps, where he still managed to play cricket. He died in 1983 at the age of ninety.

Wicketkeeper Leslie Gay played just four times for Somerset in 1894 and claimed six victims before, surprisingly, finding himself in England's Test team in Australia that winter. A noted soccer player, he appeared in goal for England and his claim to fame therefore is that he kept for his country in two sports.

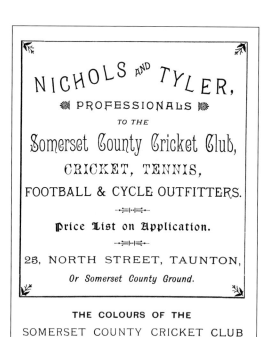

A couple of hard-working professionals who did much of Somerset's bowling in the county's early championship years, George Nichols and Ted Tyler were also partners off the field – they ran a sports shop together in Taunton. Tyler also had other businesses, including a tobacconist's, a travel agency and a pub.

George Nichols, who was a fast bowler through the 1890s, took 291 first-class wickets for Somerset after a brief spell with Gloucestershire. Sometimes he was handy with the bat as well. Once he hit a very quick 311 not out for Somerset and Ground against Glastonbury. Nichols had a flair for dramatics and a play of his was produced on the London stage.

A slow left-arm bowler relying on flight rather than spin, Ted Tyler took 864 wickets at a cost of just over 22 apiece for Somerset. He was so slow that although called for throwing no one seemed to worry. He once took all 10 Surrey wickets for 49 runs and had a single Test appearance in South Africa. While coaching at Taunton School, Tyler is credited with having realised the promise of 'Farmer' White (see pages 38 and 39).

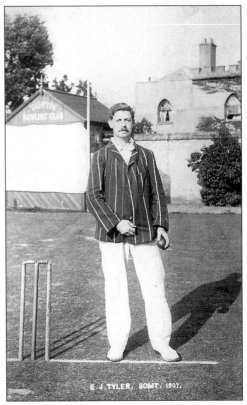

E.J.TYLER, SOMT. 1907.

A professional soldier who was decorated in both the Boer War and the First World War, Colonel Sir Walter Hedley also managed to play 84 matches for Somerset between 1892 and 1904, taking 254 wickets at under 21 apiece, including 14 for 70 against Yorkshire. His bowling action, however, was suspect, and after it was condemned at a meeting of county captains in 1900, he played little more first-class cricket.

Surrey let him go after three seasons and Somerset welcomed Len Braund. He ranks as one of the county's greatest all-rounders, as a batsman, leg-spinner, and phenomenal slip fielder. Four times he achieved the double of 1,000 runs and 100 wickets and he played in 23 Tests. Later, he became an umpire.

John Daniell equalled Sammy Woods' record of thirteen seasons as Somerset's captain, following him and leading the county either side of the First World War. He was a tough, autocratic captain who scored over 10,000 first-class runs – nearly all for Somerset. At the age of forty-six, he hit two centuries in a match against Essex at Taunton. He captained England at rugby, and was an England selector for both sports.

When Sammy Woods retired as captain, a fund was launched for his benefit. It raised £1,650 and, during the first home match of 1907 at Taunton, a cheque and illuminated address were handed to him.

One writer fairly summed up Ernie Robson as representing the best of honest professional toil on the cricket field. Between the ages of twenty-five and fifty-three, he took 1,122 first-class wickets with his medium-pace bowling and hit 12,427 runs. Aged forty-eight, he bowled unchanged in both Derbyshire innings; he hit his first century at the age of fifty and took five Essex wickets in an innings during his last year. 'Robbo' – Somerset's oldest player ever – died in 1924, shortly before he was due to become an umpire.

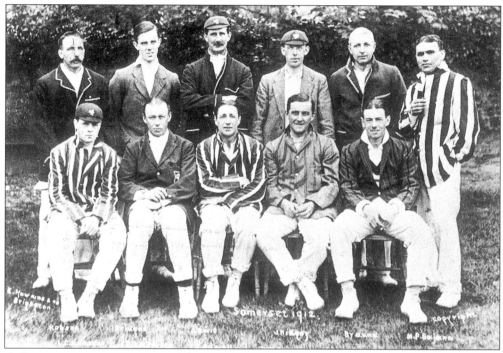

A Somerset XI in 1912. From left to right, back row: E. Robson, J. Bridges, A.E. Lewis, H. Chidgey, L. Braund, M.P. Bajana. Front row: L. Sutton, E.S.M. Poyntz, J. Daniell (*captain*), W.T. Greswell, and J. MacBryan. Poyntz took over as captain for 1913 and 1914.

At least ten Somerset cricketers lost their lives in the First World War. Let Frederick Banes-Walker represent them here. An attacking batsman, he played five times for the county in 1914, with a top score of 40. A Second Lieutenant in the Devonshire Regiment, he was killed near Ypres on 9 May 1915, aged twenty-six.

Two
Gentlemen and Players

Somerset relied on amateurs more than any other first-class county through the inter-war years and, although much more likely to be in the bottom half of the championship table than the top, were a popular and entertaining side with more than their fair share of interesting characters. Amateurs and professionals (gentlemen and players) would have had separate dressing rooms, separate gates onto the field and would arrange themselves in team photographs according to their status.

As late as 1936, Somerset used thirty-five players in one season, of whom just seven were professionals. The amateurs included one of the great names in Somerset cricket – 'Farmer' Jack White, who captained country as well as county and is remembered as one of cricket's great slow left-arm bowlers.

Two other cherished names from those years, and every boy's idols, were Arthur Wellard and Harold Gimblett, both very much professional players. Their cricket was to be interrupted for six years by the Second World War.

SOMERSET
COUNTY CRICKET CLUB.

LIST OF FIXTURES FOR 1919.

Date.	Opponents.	Where played.
May Friday 16th, Saturday 17th	SURREY - -	OVAL
May Wednesday 21st, Thursday 22nd	SUSSEX - -	TAUNTON
June Monday 9th, Tuesday 10th	GLOUCESTERSHIRE	TAUNTON
July Monday 7th, Tuesday 8th	WORCESTERSHIRE -	WORCESTER
July Wednesday 9th, Thursday 10th	DERBYSHIRE - -	DERBY
July Friday 18th, Saturday 19th	ESSEX - - -	LEYTON
July Monday 21st, Tuesday 22nd	WORCESTERSHIRE -	BATH
July Wednesday 23rd, Thursday 24th	DERBYSHIRE - -	BATH
Aug. Saturday 2nd	⚬GLASTONBURY & DISTRICT	GLASTONBURY
Aug. Monday 4th, Tuesday 5th,	GLOUCESTERSHIRE	BRISTOL
Aug. Friday 8th, Saturday 9th	HAMPSHIRE - -	WESTON
Aug. Monday 11th, Tuesday 12th	ESSEX - -	WESTON
Aug. Wednesday 13th, Thursday 14th	SUSSEX - -	BRIGHTON
Aug. Friday 15th, Saturday 16th	HAMPSHIRE - -	BOURNEM'TH
Aug. Wednesday 27th, Thursday 28th	SURREY - -	TAUNTON
Aug. Friday 29th, Saturday 30th	AUSTRALIAN I.F. XI.	TAUNTON

※ Club and Ground Match.

Season Tickets, to admit to Ground only on all County Match Days, 5/- each.

Members' Tickets, 21s., available from May 1st to September 30th, 1919, admit to the County Ground and Pavilion, Taunton, on all occasions when Cricket is being played, and to all County Matches in Somerset. Non-Transferable Extra Tickets, admitting to matches only for Members of Subscriber's Family residing under his roof, 10s. each. These may be obtained of Messrs. Fox, Fowler and Co.'s Bank, Taunton; or of Messrs. Hammett & Co., Booksellers, North Street, Taunton.

In the first season after the First World War, matches were of two days only. Somerset had fifteen first-class fixtures, with just one in June, and only thirty days' cricket altogether.

Somerset's Rippon twins – Dudley (second left) and Sydney – flanked by Northamptonshire's Denton twins. The Rippons, who were opening batsmen, made their debut in 1914. Dudley retired in 1920, troubled by a war wound, but by then had two centuries to his credit. Sydney, who had also been wounded, played his last game in 1937, having hit six centuries in his career. The twins delighted in confusing spectators and scorers, even swapping identities on occasions. Their captain, John Daniell, once described them as 'A couple of bloody lunatics'.

Wally Luckes served Somerset well behind the stumps from 1924 to 1949 and twice he did not concede a bye when Somerset's opponents topped 500. He is second only to Harold Stephenson in the number of dismissals by a Somerset wicketkeeper. Nearly a third of his 827 victims were stumped.

Reggie Ingle, a Bath solicitor, played over 300 matches for Somerset between the wars and notched almost 10,000 runs, twice getting 1,000 in a season. He captained the county for six summers in the 1930s, and was well liked and respected by the professionals.

A hard-hitting batsman, E.S. Massey Poyntz's first-class career dates from 1909 until 1919, and he captained Somerset twice. He came from a cricketing family. Brother Hugh occasionally played for the county until 1921, his appearances restricted by his service as a regular Army officer.

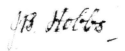

Hammett & Co., Printers, Parade, Taunton.

COUNTY CRICKET GROUND, TAUNTON.

Saturday, Monday and Tuesday, August 15th, 17th and 18th, 1925,

SOMERSET v. SURREY

FIRST INNINGS.	SOMERSET.	SECOND INNINGS.
1 J. C. W. MacBryan b Holmes .. 6	b Fender	109
2 Young c Sadler b Lockton 58	c Strudwick b Sadler	 71
3 T. E. S. Francis b Sadler .. 0	c Strudwick b Lockton	 12
4 J. C. White b Sadler 1	c Strudwick b Sadler	 30
5 P. R. Johnson c & b Lockton 30	c Peach b Fender	 16
6 E. F. Longrigg b Sadler 5	run out	 4
7 R. A. Ingle b Fender 22	c Shepherd b Peach	 23
8 Hunt b Lockton 4	b Fender	 59
9 J. Bridges c & b Shepherd 25	b Fender	 26
10 R. G. R.-Glasgow c Jardine b Lockton 4	c Sadler b Fender	 5
11 M. Ll.-Hill not out 0	not out	 1
b, 1-b8, n-b, w4 .. 12	b9, 1-b5, n-b4, w	.. 18

Total ..167

Total ..374

1-11 2-12 3-16 4-93 5-110 6-112 7-118 8-126 9-163 10-167
1-184 2-203 3-228 4-262 5-268 6-268 7-310 8-352 9-373 10-374

FIRST INNINGS.	SURREY.	SECOND INNINGS.
1 Hobbs c Hill b Bridges 101	not out	101
2 Sandham c Longrigg b Bridges .. 13	not out	 74
3 D. J. Knight run out 34	....	
4 Shepherd b White 0	....	
5 D. R. Jardine run out 47	....	
6 E. R. T. Holmes c Hill b Glasgow .. 24	....	
7 P. G. H. Fender st. Hill b Young .. 59	....	
8 Peach b Young 20	....	
9 J. H. Lockton absent	....	
10 Sadler c Johnson b Young 25	....	
11 Strudwick not out 10	....	
b15, 1-b8, n-b3, w .. 26	b7, 1-b1, n-b, w	.. 8

Total .. 359

Total ..183

1-50 2-146 3-148 4-170 5-221 6-260 7-322 8-325 9-359 10-
1- 2- 3- 4- 5- 6- 7- 8- 9- 10-

Scorers—Trump & Boyington.   Umpires—Draper & Young.

Lunch Interval 1.30 p.m.   Tea Interval 4.15 p.m.   Stumps Drawn 5.30 p.m.

BOWLING ANALYSIS.

SOMERSET.

	First Innings.				Second Innings.			
	O.	M.	R.	W.	O.	M.	R.	W.
P. G. H. Fender ...	13	3	39	1	35·5	8	120	5
E. R. T. Holmes ...	6	2	12	1	17	—	56	—
J. H. Lockton ...	16	4	36	4	9	2	15	1
Sadler	16	4	28	3	21	5	59	2
Peach	9	2	21	—	20	7	46	1
Shepherd ...	6·3	1	19	1	21	5	60	—

Sadler bowled 2 wides.

Mr. Fender and Mr. Holmes bowled 1 wide each.

Mr. Fender bowled 3 no-balls.

Mr. Holmes bowled 1 no-ball.

SURREY.

	First Innings.				Second Innings.			
	O.	M.	R.	W.	O.	M.	R.	W.
J. C. White ...	29	13	61	1	14	6	34	—
R.-Glasgow ...	26	1	144	1	6	—	42	—
J. J. Bridges ...	37	5	115	2	11	3	27	—
Hunt	4	1	14	—	8	4	15	—
Young	5·3	1	9	3	15·5	1	39	—
E. F. Longrigg ...	—	—	—	—	3	—	18	—

Mr. R.-Glasgow bowled 3 no-balls.

Creating Two Records by J. B. HOBBS.

126th and 127th Centuries.

15th and 14th Centuries in One Season.

Taunton attracted a big crowd and an unusual number of reporters and photographers for the Surrey match in 1925. They cheered Jack Hobbs as he equalled W.G. Grace's total of 126 first-class centuries, and those who stayed for the second innings saw him score another.

The roll of Somerset cricketers includes twenty pairs of brothers (three in the case of the Ebdon family in the 1890s) and eight instances of fathers and sons playing for the county. The latter category includes Dickie Burrough, who had 171 matches between 1927 and 1947, whilst his father, William, had managed just four. Dickie, a solicitor at Bath, averaged just over 20 with the bat.

Another Bath lawyer, 'Bunty' Longrigg, captained Somerset either side of the Second World War and, in 1946, led the county to fourth place. He hit 205 against Leicester at Taunton in 1930 and totalled over 8,000 runs. He later served the club as chairman and president.

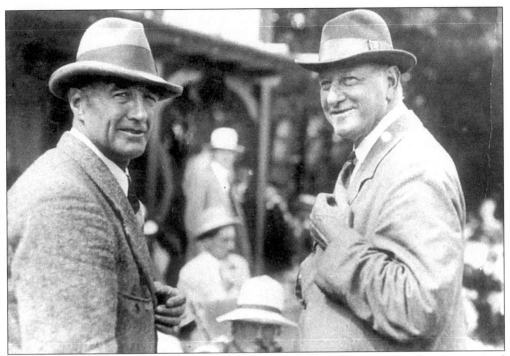

Two old-timers with plenty to talk about: John Daniell (left) and Sammy Woods each captained Somerset at cricket for thirteen seasons and they both captained England at rugby.

C.C.C. Case (the initials stand for Cecil Charles Coles) was almost thirty when he first played for Somerset in 1925. A dour, defensive batsman, he was very hard to dislodge. 'Box' Case was among the more valuable amateurs in the side. He hit 1,000 runs in three of his eleven seasons, and he and J.C. White set a Somerset record with a fifth-wicket stand of 235.

One of the game's great slow left-arm bowlers, John Cornish White looked like a Somerset farmer – which was what he was. He played for the county between 1909 and 1937 and was captain for five seasons. He totalled 2,166 wickets for Somerset (a lot more than anyone else) and they cost only 18 runs apiece. White captained England too, in four of his fifteen Tests. His total first-class wicket haul was 2,356.

White was no mean bat, either. He twice hit 1,000 runs in a season, and totalled 11,000 runs in his county career. There were six centuries, including 192 off Nottinghamshire at Taunton.

APRIL				
un.	7	14	21	28
Mon.	1	8	15	22	29
ues.	2	9	16	23	30
Wed.	3	10	17	24
h.	4	11	18	25
ri.	5	12	19	26
at.	6	13	20	27

DAILY SKETCH

TUESDAY, APRIL 23, 1929   Head Office: 200, Gray's Inn-road, W.C.1.   'Phone: Museum 9841.

SOMERSET MEN CHEER 'FARMER WHITE'

'Farmer' White, as he was often called, was a national hero in the 1928/29 Tests in Australia, playing a big role in England's Ashes triumph. When he returned, a great crowd, including Taunton's Mayor and MP, met him at the railway station and joined a procession through the town. In the fourth Test at Adelaide, in sweltering heat, White bowled 124.5 overs and took 13 wickets for 256 runs.

Relying more on flight and change of pace than spin, White produced many remarkable match figures for Somerset. In one day at Bath in 1919, he took 16 Worcestershire wickets for 83 runs and, two years later against the same county at Worcester, he claimed all 10 in an innings.

39

For half a century, Cecil Buttle was assistant or head groundsman and he was awarded a testimonial in 1972. He was also a useful medium-pace bowler and had two first-class matches in the mid-1920s.

Making his Somerset debut at sixteen in 1931, Norman Mitchell-Innes played for England at the age of twenty, while still at Oxford. It was his only Test, for he withdrew from a second because of hay fever and was not picked again. His job in the Sudan Political Service restricted his Somerset career, but he hit 1,000 runs three times and was joint captain in 1948.

The Lee brothers – Frank (left) and Jack – made their careers with Somerset, leaving a third brother, Harry, playing for Middlesex (for whom they each had a game or two). They opened together many times and, in three successive innings, put on 213, 119 and 146 for the first wicket. Jack, whose career spanned from 1925 until 1936, became groundsman and coach at Millfield School. He was killed in action in Normandy in June 1944. In his earlier years, he had also been a professional footballer. Frank, a left-hander, proved an ideal partner for Somerset's new opener, Harold Gimblett. He hit twenty-three centuries for Somerset and averaged nearly 28. Frank became an umpire in 1948 and stood in 29 Tests. Brother Harry, also an opener, played 401 matches for Middlesex.

Jake Seamer, like Mitchell-Innes, earned his living in the Sudan Political Service, which restricted his appearances for Somerset to 59 during the 1930s and for a year or two after the war. He was good at 'holding the fort' and his highest score was 70. He shared the Somerset captaincy with no fewer than four others in his last season, 1948. Seamer once hit a century before breakfast, but that was in the Sudan, when the cricket started at 7 a.m.

41

To be a fast bowler and then hit lots of sixes is the dream of many boys. For all those, and their fathers, who did not realise the dream there was always Arthur Wellard to show them how to do it – and with a wide grin as well. He took over 1,500 wickets in nearly 400 matches as a professional with Somerset, and totalled 172 in the 1938 season.

It was his bowling that earned Wellard a couple of Tests in the late 1930s (war ended his chance of more), but it is as a big hitter that he is as well remembered. A quarter of his 12,000 runs came from sixes. On two occasions he hit sixes off five successive balls – both times at Wells. In 1935 he struck sixty-six sixes, a record number over a season until Ian Botham came along. Wellard is also remembered as a brave fielder at silly mid-off, long before helmets were introduced.

42

Taking the field against Lancashire at Weston-super-Mare in 1935. From left to right: H.D. Burrough, J.W. Lee (hidden), W.T. Luckes, F.S. Lee, A. Wellard, N.S. Mitchell-Innes, W. Andrews, R.A. Ingle, J.H. Cameron, H. Gimblett, and H.L. Hazell.

Somerset Cricket has seen many colourful characters. High among their ranks is R.J.O. Meyer, the founder of Millfield School, who played between 1936 and 1949. There are stories galore of his eccentric and unorthodox ways, but they should not overshadow the fact that he was a fine cricketer who could have become a very good one indeed. He averaged 28 with the bat (his innings included an undefeated double century) and took 158 wickets with a mixture of deliveries (sometimes, it is said, six different ones in a single over).

43

Cricket at Bath between the wars. The city has a long and close involvement in the Somerset cricket story. The first first-class match at the recreation ground there was a century ago.

Very much a man of Bath (though born in Bristol), Bertie Buse worked in a solicitor's office and played for Somerset as an amateur before turning professional. He was a valued member of the team, scoring 1,000 runs in five seasons and taking over 650 wickets in all with his medium-pace bowling. His career spanned from 1929 to 1953. Buse also played rugby for the county.

Only four Somerset bowlers have taken more wickets for the county than Horace Hazell, who claimed 957 victims with his slow left-arm spin during the 1930s and a few post-war seasons. He had a remarkable spell against Gloucester at Taunton in 1949, bowling 17.3 overs (105 deliveries) without conceding a run.

A cartoon produced for Hazell's benefit year, featuring some of his team-mates.

Harold Gimblett (left) shares a photograph with Alan Pearse, who had played alongside him in the Watchett CC team and was now making the first of a handful of appearances for Somerset. It was the previous year, 1935, that Gimblett had made his own county debut in sensational fashion. Turned down after a trial, the twenty-year-old farmer's son was called up unexpectedly to fill a place in Somerset's side against Essex at Frome. He hitched a lift, and went in at number eight with the score at 107 for 6. With a borrowed bat he then hit the fastest century of the summer in 63 minutes.

'The most exciting batsman of his day' Wisden said of Gimblett, Somerset's new opener. Between 1935 and 1954 he scored more first-class runs for the county than anyone else before or since: 21,142 at an average of 36.96. Twice, he scored 2,000 in a season. All but one of his fifty centuries were for Somerset. For nearly forty years, his 310 off Sussex in 1948 stood as a record for the county.

TELEGRAMS,
LORD'S GROUND LONDON.
TELEPHONE Nº
ABERCORN 2241 (PAVILION)
ABERCORN 1838 (TENNIS COURT)
ABERCORN 3386 (HOTEL)

SECRETARY—LT.-COL. R. S. RAIT KERR
ASST. SECRETARY—R. AIRD

Lord's Cricket Ground,
London, N.W. 8.

Dear *Gimblett*

    The Board of Control Selection Committee will be glad if you will ~~be ready to~~ play, ~~if selected~~, for England against the West Indies at Lord's on June 24th, 26th & 27th.

    Play will begin at 11.30 a.m. on the first day and 11 a.m. on the second and third days.

    The Board of Control has laid it down that when inviting a cricketer to play, the Selection Committee shall make it a condition in writing that the cricketer does not contribute a report or statement of any kind to the Press, or give any broadcast talk or statement, until the end of the season, as regards any Test Match for which he is selected and in which he plays.

    The remuneration of each professional will be £27. 10. 0d, 12th man £20, reserve men £18, plus 3rd class railway fares in each case.

    Hotel bills, excluding drinks, will be paid by the Board of Control in the case of all professionals who stay at the Great Central Hotel, Marylebone, which is the Hotel nominated by the Selection Committee. Everyone is expected to stay at the Great Central Hotel, except those who are being put up privately or are staying at home.

    Each player is entitled to two Complimentary tickets for the match for his friends. These should be applied for in writing to the Secretary of the M.C.C., Lord's Cricket Ground, N.W. 8.

                    Yours faithfully,

                   P. Perrin

            Chairman, Selection Committee.

                                R.330.

Cautious selectors were not too sure about Gimblett, and he had only three Tests. This letter called him up for the Lord's Test against the West Indians in 1939.

SOM BY. WON INNS & 72 RUNS *(handwritten annotation)*

Somerset v. West Indies 1939.

Wednesday, Thursday and Friday, August 2nd 3rd and 4th, 1939.

WEST INDIES.	FIRST INNINGS.		SECOND INNINGS.	
1 J. B. Stollmeyer	not out	45	c Gimblett b Meyer	8
2 V. H. Stollmeyer	l-b-w b Andrews	2	b Wellard	14
3 G. H. Headley	l-b-w b Wellard	0	l-b-w b Wellard	31
4 K. H. Weekes	b Andrews	4	c & b Hazell	54
5 J. E. D. Sealy	b Andrews	0	c Bennett b Meyer	1
6 L. N. Constantine	c Buse b Andrews	4	b Hazell	10
*7 J. H. Cameron	b Wellard	17	absent hurt	0
‡8 I. Barrow	c Luckes b Andrews	4	c Hazell b Meyer	29
9 E. A. Williams	b Wellard	3	not out	29
10 C. B. Clarke	b Wellard	4	c Gimblett b Hazell	4
11 T. Johnson	b Andrews	0	b Hazell	2
	b, l-b, w, n-b1, ...	1	b4, l-b3, w, n-b, ...	7
	Total ...	84	Total ...	189

Fall of the wickets

1-11 2-12 3-19 4-25 5-29 6-50 7-55 8-68 9 81 10-84
1-22 2-22 3-24 4-88 5-119 6-124 7-170 8-175 9-189 10-

BOWLING ANALYSIS. Name.	First Innings. O.	M.	R.	W.	Wd.	N-b.	Second Innings. O.	M.	R.	W.	Wd.	N-b.
Wellard	16	3	43	4	...		22	3	78	2	...	...
Andrews	16	4	40	6	...	1	7	0	10		...	...
MEYER	...	...	...	...	...	...	12	5	20	3	...	...
HAZELL	...	...	...	...	...	...	15.4	1	74	4	...	...
	...	...	...	...	...	...	...	...	...	...	...	...

SOMERSET.	FIRST INNINGS.		SECOND INNINGS.
1 Lee (F. S.)	b Johnson	7	
2 Gimblett	l-b-w b Williams	11	
3 Buse	l-b-w b Clarke	21	
4 R. J. O. Meyer	c Barrow b Clarke	78	
*5 E. F. Longrigg	c Williams b Clarke	16	
6 F. M. McRae	l-b-w b Constantine	34	
‡7 Luckes	not out	71	
8 G. M. Bennett	c Barrow b Clarke	56	
9 Andrews	c sub. b Clarke	18	
10 Wellard	c Sealy b Constantine	18	
11 Hazell	b Clarke	1	
	b11, l-b3, w, n-b, ...	14	b, l-b, w, n-b, ...
	Total ...	345	Total ...

Fall of the wickets

1-7 2-33 3-49 4-97 5-164 6-176 7 289 8-321 9-343 10-345
1- 2- 3- 4- 5- 6- 7- 8- 9- 10-

BOWLING ANALYSIS. Name.	First Innings. O.	M.	R.	W.	Wd.	N-b.	Second Innings. O.	M.	R.	W.	Wd.	N-b.
Constantine	23	2	98	2	...	...	...	...	...	...	...	...
Johnson	11	2	38	1	...	...	...	...	...	...	...	...
Williams	11	1	44	1	...	...	...	...	...	...	...	...
Clarke	24.2	4	138	6	...	...	...	...	...	...	...	...
Sealy	2	...	13	...	...	...	...	...	...	...	...	...
	...	...	...	...	...	...	...	...	...	...	...	...

Scorers—R. Trump & W. Ferguson.   Umpires—G. Beet & J. Newman.
Hours of Play—1st day 11.30—7.   2nd day 11.30—7.   3rd day 11.15—4.45 or 5.15
      Lunch Interval—1.30—2.10.   Tea Interval—subject to state of game.
West Indies won the toss.   * Captain.   ‡ Wicket keeper.   P.T.O.

A feat unlikely to be repeated – Somerset beat the West Indies by an innings.

Those in the back row were the professionals, whilst the amateurs were at the front of this photograph of Somerset's team that faced Middlesex at Bath in 1938. From left to right, back row: H. Hazell, W.T. Luckes, W. Andrews, H.F.T. Buse, F.S. Lee, H. Gimblett. Front row: L. St V. Powell, R.A. Ingle, E.F. Longrigg, M.D. Lyon, and H.D. Burrough.

If an eleven of the county's greatest characters were selected, Bill Andrews (1930-47) would be sure of a place. Gregarious, impetuous and sometimes exasperating, he was a man with a fund of stories. Twice sacked as a player and twice as a coach, he had a wholehearted devotion to Somerset cricket. Andrews and Wellard were a formidable pair of opening bowlers and, but for the war, he might also have played for England. Twice he achieved the double, and he took a total of 750 wickets and hit nearly 5,000 runs for the county. (See also page 123.)

49

Somerset County Cricket Club

Full conditions of membership will be found on pages 20 and 21.

Subscription

21/-

which entitles the Member to purchase

Family Tickets

at the rate of

12/6

carrying full Membership privileges.

Membership of the Club for the past eleven years.		
Year.	*Members.*	*Family.*
1928	2,390	1,020
1929	2,347	1,014
1930	2,317	1,012
1931	2,107	828
1932	1,931	727
1933	1,924	765
1934	1,928	756
1935	1,861	653
1936	1,877	562
1937	1,904	522
1938	2,041	630

Sixteen Matches in Somerset:

TAUNTON	·	·	·	7
WESTON	·	·	·	3
BATH	·	·	·	3
FROME	·	·	·	1
YEOVIL	·	·	·	1
WELLS	·	·	·	1

Members can also obtain

TRANSFERABLE TICKETS

at the rate of £1 1s. 0d. each.

These Transferable Tickets carry all the privileges of Membership— except the right of voting at Annual or Special General Meetings.

A membership recruitment leaflet, produced just before the Second World War.

Three

After the War

The first year of peace, 1946, was a good one for Somerset, who gained twelve championship victories and finished fourth in the table. But it was soon back to the bottom half of the table. In 1952, and for the next three seasons, they were in last place.

It was one of those times in Somerset's history when lack of resources both on and off the field seemed to threaten the club's ability to stay among the first-class counties. In 1953, a revolt was led by three well-known local journalists with a passion for Somerset cricket against what was seen as complacency by the establishment. Many members backed them and the 'rebels' gained a voice on the county committee. New ideas were put forward and gradually changes came.

The club was soon to have its first professional captain, Maurice Tremlett (a few years before his appointment at the helm, no fewer than five amateurs had led the team in a single season). Talent was recruited from Commonwealth countries, which led to Somerset being dubbed the 'League of Nations'.

Somerset C.C.C. 1946

Somerset in 1946, when, led by 'Bunty' Longrigg, they had one of their most successful seasons. From left to right, back row: H. Gimblett, F.S. Lee, A. Wellard, R. Trump (*scorer*), W.R. Andrews, H.F.T. Buse, J. Lawrence. Front row: W.T. Luckes, A.T.W. Jones, N.S. Mitchell-Innes, E.F. Longrigg, C.J.P. Barnwell, G.R. Langdale.

A diminutive man with a great relish for the game, Johnny Lawrence was a leg-break bowler who took 100 wickets in a season twice and scored 1,000 runs three times. Altogether he took almost 800 wickets and hit over 9,000 runs in his years with the county after the war. In his last season (1955) he achieved the hat-trick against his native Yorkshire.

There were plenty of autograph opportunities for the youngsters on this occasion around half a century ago, thought to be a match at a local club in aid of the benefit year of either Bill Andrews (second left) in 1948, or Horace Hazell (second right) in 1949. Maurice Tremlett (right) and Harold Stephenson were also in the match.

Stuart Rogers, one of Somerset's last amateur captains, led the county at the age of twenty-seven in 1950 and for the next two seasons. In the war he had served in Burma with the Chindits. An attacking batsman, he hit three centuries and once reached 1,000 runs in a season. He died at the age of forty-six.

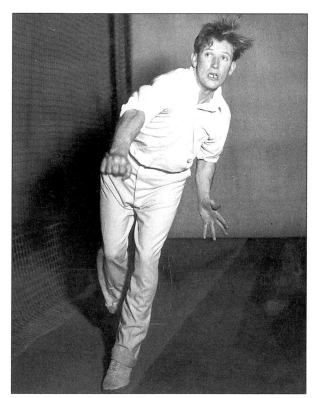

In 1956, Maurice Tremlett made Somerset cricket history by becoming its first professional captain, a job he did well for four seasons. He had made the headlines on his debut in 1947 with a match-winning performance against the mighty Middlesex side at Lord's. The twenty-four-year-old newcomer destroyed the home side with a spell of 5 wickets for 8 runs in five overs of pace and then, with the bat, saw Somerset to a one-wicket victory. The Middlesex men lined up to applaud him off the field.

That winter Tremlett went to the West Indies and played, with little success, in three Tests. Sadly, he lost his way as a bowler – not at all helped by advice he was given at the time. Instead he blossomed as a batsman, scoring over 15,000 runs (including fifteen centuries) for Somerset, and hit 1,000 runs in a season nine times. He took 326 wickets for the county.

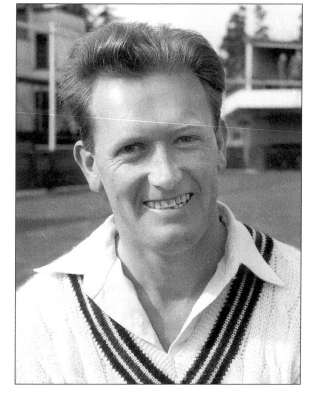

Taking the field against
Glamorgan at Neath in 1949.
From left to right: H.F.T. Buse,
E. Hill, G.E.S. Woodhouse
(*captain*), H. Gimblett,
A. Wellard, J. Lawrence (partly
hidden), H.W. Stephenson,
S.S. Rogers, M.F. Tremlett,
M. Coope, H.L. Hazell.

Micky Walford hit an unbeaten
century on his debut for Somerset
against the Indians at Taunton in
1946 and, the following summer,
took 264 off Hampshire at
Weston-super-Mare. A
schoolmaster, his county cricket
was confined mainly to August,
otherwise he would have played a
lot more than his 52 matches – in
which he averaged over 40. He
was a triple blue at Oxford
(cricket, rugby, and hockey), and
captained the England hockey
team.

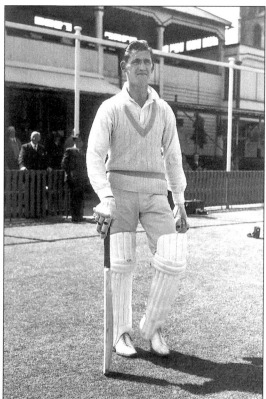

A professional captain was still a year away, and the Royal Navy obliged by releasing their leading cricketer, Gerry Tordoff, for the summer of 1955 so that he could lead Somerset as an amateur. A pugnacious left-handed batsman, he hit 1,000 runs in that season and one other.

Somerset's recruitment of overseas players to strengthen the side in the 1950s led to the county being dubbed the 'League of Nations'. Yawar Saeed was one such imported player. He took 78 wickets in his three seasons. Back home he played for the Punjab and later he became a selector for Pakistan.

A Somerset XI in 1952. From left to right, back row: R. Trump (*scorer*), R. Smith, H.W. Stephenson, J. Redman, F.L. Angell, D.L. Kitson, J. Lawrence. Front row: M.F. Tremlett, G.B. Brocklehurst, S.S. Rogers (*captain*), H. Gimblett, H.F.T. Buse, E.P. Robinson.

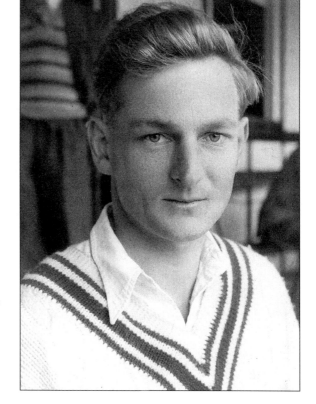

Farmer Ben Brocklehurst played for three seasons (from 1952 until 1954), spending the last two as captain. With Somerset at a very low ebb on and off the field during this time, it was hardly an enviable job, as Gerry Tordoff, his successor, also found. Brocklehurst scored 1,671 runs.

Some Somerset cricketing personalities pictured in mufti in the 1950s. From left to right: Les Angell, Peter Wight, 'Bunty' Longrigg, Harold Stephenson, John Barnwell, Ken Palmer, Richard Robinson (*club secretary*).

Over the years, the Somerset Second XI has been the proving ground for many would-be-first-class players. Almost all of those in this 1955 photograph played for the first team at some time. From left to right, back row: Peter Eele, Terry Lovell, Graham Atkinson, Ken Palmer, Jim Hilton, Clive Davey, Bill Andrews (*coach*). Front row: Ken Biddulph, John Baker, Roy Smith, Eric Hill, John Currie, Lloyd Williams, Philip Fussell.

Somerset taking the field at Morlands, Glastonbury, 1956. They are being led by Maurice Tremlett, in his first year as captain.

Chris Greetham was immaculate in his appearance, played handsome shots and was a useful bowler (as well as a superb cover point). More than one writer has lamented that he was not around to play more one-day cricket. In his 205 matches (between 1957 and 1966) he scored nearly 7,000 runs and took almost 200 wickets. In 1963, he and Harold Stephenson set a ninth-wicket record of 183.

Somerset County Cricket Club

COUNTY CRICKET CLUB,

TAUNTON.

Dear Sir or Madam,

A TESTIMONIAL has been granted to C. L. McCool during the coming season.

Although 'Colin' McCool has played for the County for only three seasons he has made a valuable contribution as an all-rounder.

In this period, due in part to his experience and enthusiasm, the County has improved from 15th to 3rd position in the Championship Table.

His figures for the Club are:—

BATTING

Innings 160, Not out 6, Total runs 4994, Highest score 169, Average 32.42

BOWLING

Overs 1219.4, Maidens 230, Runs 3617, Wickets 128, Average 28.25

WICKET KEEPING—Caught 2, Stumped 1

Catches 97.   Centuries 6

A short description of his previous cricket career is given below:—

Played for New South Wales 1939-40 to 1941-42, and Queensland 1945-46. Tests for Australia (14), v. New Zealand 1945-46, v. England 1946-47, v. South Africa 1949-50 and v. India 1947-48.   Toured England 1948-49 and South Africa 1949-50.   Professional for East Lancashire and Stockport.

The Committee hopes that Members will subscribe generously to make this Testimonial a great success.

When sending your donation please include on remittance slip.

R. ROBINSON,

Secretary.

A testimonial leaflet for one of Somerset's 'League of Nations' men.

Third place in the table for these 1958 players. From left to right, back row: B. Roe, B.A. Langford, C.H.M. Greetham, B. Lobb, K.D. Biddulph, E. Bryant, W.E. Alley, T. Tout (*scorer*). Front row: J.G. Lomax, C.L. McCool, M.F. Tremlett, H.W. Stephenson, P.B. Wight.

Australian all-rounder Colin McCool, with 14 Tests behind him, was forty when he joined Somerset in 1956 and he stayed for five seasons. He proved particularly valuable with the bat, scoring a total of nearly 8,000 runs at an average of 33.81. He also claimed 219 victims with his leg-break bowling.

Peter Wight came to Somerset in 1953 from British Guyana via Lancashire League cricket and hit a century off the Australians on his debut for the county. A slim, stylish batsman, he scored nearly 17,000 runs with twenty-seven centuries (including an unbeaten double century off Kent at Taunton). In 1966, he started a long new career as a first-class umpire.

Another Australian with Somerset in the 1950s was John McMahon, a reliable slow left-arm bowler who had previously had a few years with Surrey. He took 349 wickets in his four seasons. His best figures for Somerset were 8 for 46, which he returned against Kent at Yeovil in 1955. Seven years earlier, he had recorded the same bowling figures for Surrey *v*. Northamptonshire at the Oval.

Harold Stephenson took over the captaincy in 1960. This team from that year was, from left to right, back row: R. Virgin, F.J. Herting, K.D. Biddulph, T. Tout (*scorer*), A.G.T. Whitehead, K.E. Palmer, G. Atkinson. Front row: A.A. Baig, M. Tremlett, H.W. Stephenson, C.L. McCool, B.A. Langford, P.B. Wight.

Somerset would have liked Dennis Silk to have been in their team a lot more often, but only 33 of his 83 first-class matches were for the county (and only one of his seven centuries). A reliable bat, he averaged nearly 34 for Somerset. He played many matches for MCC and took part in four overseas tours, actually captaining two of them (North America and New Zealand). A top headmaster, he became president of MCC after retiring to Somerset.

A montage of photographs from Weston-super-Mare in 1963.

Ken Palmer on his way to Leeds for the Test against the West Indies in 1963, when he was twelfth man. An opening bat in his early days with Somerset, he was to take 837 wickets at just over 21 apiece – including nine in an innings at Trent Bridge in 1963. He claimed 100 wickets in a season on four occasions with his fast-medium deliveries. He had just one Test appearance in South Africa. Ken became an umpire, as did brother Roy, who also bowled for Somerset (and did the hat-trick in a Sunday League match). Ken's son, Gary, also played for the county during the 1980s.

After Warwickshire let him go, Bryan Lobb joined Somerset and went on, in 1957, to become the county's first fast bowler since the war to take 100 wickets in a season (for under 20 runs apiece). His appearances were less frequent when he became a schoolmaster, his Somerset career tally of wickets being 368.

In a first-class career that spanned over twenty years, Brian Langford notched up several records. He started in 1953 at Bath, aged seventeen, with 26 victims in three matches with his off-spin. Five years later, he became Somerset's youngest player to claim 100 in a season. He played in 504 first-class matches – more than any other Somerset man – and only White and Wellard took more than his total of 1,390 wickets. Once, in a Sunday League match, he bowled eight overs without conceding a run. Langford captained Somerset for three summers.

As well as its overseas newcomers, Somerset recruited from other counties while in the doldrums during the 1950s. All-rounder Geoff Lomax, from his native Lancashire, was an important signing. He hit over 7,500 runs in his 211 matches and took over 235 wickets (including a hat-trick).

Life begins at forty, they used to say, and few sportsman can have enjoyed their forties as much as Bill Alley. Born in Sydney, he was a noted boxer and had a modest cricket career for New South Wales before nine seasons in Lancashire League games. Then, at the age of thirty-eight, he joined Somerset and his next twelve summers were incredible. An aggressive left-hand batsman and right-arm fast-medium bowler, he scored 16,644 runs (averaging over 30) and took 738 wickets at 22 apiece.

Bill Alley's greatest year was 1961, when he had an aggregate (in all first-class matches) of 3,019, including 221 not out against Warwickshire, and an average of 56.96. He reached 1,000 in ten seasons and achieved the double in 1962. A great and popular character, never lost for a word, he became an umpire when he had turned fifty.

A Somerset team early in the 1962 season. From left to right, back row: M.E. Latham, B. Roe, G. Atkinson, T. Tout (*scorer*), K.E. Palmer, M.J. Kitchen, I.R. Lomax. Front row: B.A. Langford, C.R.M. Atkinson, H.W. Stephenson (*captain*), J.G. Lomax, W.E. Alley.

Harold Stephenson played more first-class matches for the county than anyone else except Brian Langford and claimed more dismissals than any other Somerset wicketkeeper – 1,006 for the county (1,082 in all) with almost a third of those being stumpings. In one season he dismissed 86 batsman and he hit 1,000 runs five times in his career. Stephenson captained the county for five seasons and led them to third place in the table. Only Godfrey Evans kept him from a Test career.

In the space of sixteen years, Colin Atkinson was Somerset player, captain, chairman and president, and the pavilion is named after him. A Yorkshireman, he led the county to third place in 1966 and to its first Lord's final the next year. Originally a leg-spinner, he switched to seamers because of arthritis and took nearly 200 wickets in his eight playing seasons. He topped 1,000 runs once. Atkinson followed R.J.O. Meyer as Millerfield's head.

A talented Somerset XI in 1965. From left to right, back row: T. Tout (*scorer*), R.T. Virgin, K.E. Palmer, G.H. Hall, C.H.M. Greetham, G. Clayton, P.J. Robinson. Front row: P.B. Wight, B.A. Langford, C.R.M. Atkinson (*captain*), W.E. Alley, G. Atkinson.

Enough Australian cricketers have played for Somerset over the years to put together a formidable XI. The captain of this dream team would undoubtedly be Greg Chappell. He arrived in Taunton in 1968 as an unknown nineteen-year-old and hit 1,000 runs in each of his two seasons. He also scored the very first century in the Sunday League.

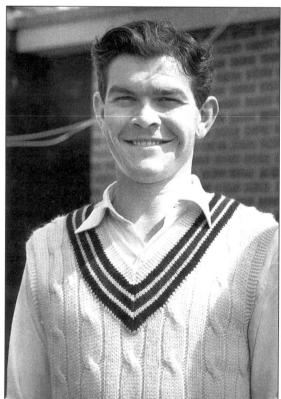

Yorkshire-born Graham Atkinson was only sixteen when he first played for Somerset and, seven years later, in 1961, became the youngest batsman to hit 2,000 in a season for the county. A sound opener, he averaged 32. After thirteen years he left to finish his career with Lancashire.

Somerset's first final at Lord's in 1967 ended in defeat by Kent. The losers are receiving their Gillette Cup runners-up medals from Sir Alec Douglas Home, president of MCC.

In 1970, Roy Virgin hit 2,223 runs for Somerset, including seven Championship centuries, and the fans hoisted 'Roy for England' banners. However, the nearest he got to a Test place was to be twelfth man. A smallish and sturdy opener, Virgin topped 1,000 runs nine times and hit twenty-two centuries for Somerset. In one season he took 42 catches. After sixteen summers he left to finish his cricket with Northamptonshire.

A photocall in 1968 – not only for the cricketers but for the club staff, too. From left to right, back row: C. Buttle, E. Woodgate, P.J. Robinson, R.T. Virgin, A. Clarkson, M.J. Kitchen, K.E. Palmer, R.A. Brooks, D. Price, D. Hunt. Middle row: R. Holman, G.I. Burgess, L.M.L. Barnwell, F.E. Rumsey, R. Palmer, G.S. Chappell, T.I. Barwell, T. Tout. Front row: Mrs A. Smith, W.E. Alley, W.H.R. Andrews, R.C. Kerslake, B.A. Langford, R. Robinson, Mrs A. Lewis.

Leaving Worcestershire in the early 1960s, Fred Rumsey soon made a big impact for Somerset with his fast left-arm deliveries. He had 100 wickets in a season for the county twice and played in five Tests. His total haul for Somerset was 520 wickets, costing under 20 runs apiece.

Four
Days of Glory

After his long career with Yorkshire, Brian Close arrived in Somerset in 1971. He became captain the following year. One cricket writer has aptly summed him up as a 'timely catalyst', and supporters sensed a new determination in the team.

The signing of Viv Richards and, later, Joel Garner coincided with the emergence of one of cricket's greatest all-rounders (and Somerset's greatest-ever player) Ian Botham, not to mention a wealth of home-grown talent – notably Brian Rose, Vic Marks, and Peter Roebuck, all future captains.

Back in 1967, Somerset had reached the final of the Gillette Cup, losing to Kent. Now Rose, succeeding Close, led the county to five titles in five years. Firstly, in 1979 Somerset won the Gillette Cup and the Sunday League; in 1981 and 1982 the Benson and Hedges Cup and, in 1983, the NatWest Trophy. At last the fans had something to cheer about.

When Brian Close and Yorkshire parted company after twenty-two years, the one-time England captain was enticed to Somerset by Bill Andrews. In his first season with his new county, Close hit five centuries and he took over the captaincy the following year (1972).

In his seven seasons with Somerset, Close averaged just under 40 and also took 74 wickets. In 1976, aged forty-five, he was recalled to the England side against the West Indians. The next season (his last) the county had a historic win over the Australians at Bath.

Viv Richards, the cricketing genius from Antigua, began his career with Somerset in 1974 and very soon it was clear that here was one of cricket's great players. That same year, he became a Test player. Apart from memorable innings in the one-day competitions, Richards had 191 first-class matches with Somerset, scoring nearly 15,000 runs, including 47 centuries, at an average of almost 50. He hit 322, Somerset's highest individual score, off Warwickshire at Taunton in 1985 and also scored five double centuries.

A young Ian Botham is seen with Len Creed, the Bath bookmaker who has the credit for bringing Viv Richards to Somerset. He had seen a brief reference in print to the West Indian and sought him out while in the Caribbean with a touring side – the Mendip Acorns. Creed was chairman of Lansdown CC, the oldest surviving Somerset club, and took Richards to Bath to play for them while qualifying for the county.

Brian Rose, who had nineteen seasons with Somerset, was a successful skipper when he led the county for six of them. It was during his reign that Somerset gained its first trophies. A talented left-hand opener, he played for England nine times. For Somerset he averaged 33 in first-class matches and his twenty-three centuries included a double century off Northamptonshire. He was Man of the Match in the defeat of the Australians at Bath.

Joel Garner (or 'Big Bird') from Barbados was one of the most unplayable fast men the game has known and made a big contribution to Somerset's successes under Rose. Apart from his key role in one-day competitions, Garner took 338 first-class wickets for Somerset at 18 runs apiece and once hit 90 with the bat.

SOMERSET COUNTY CRICKET CLUB
Somerset v. Australians
Played at Bath on May 18th, 19th and 20th, 1977

Somerset won by seven wickets
The Australians won the toss and batted

Australians

	First Innings		Second Innings	
R. B. McCosker	c Botham b Garner	2	run out	2
C. S. Serjeant	st Taylor b Burgess	13	c Garner b Botham	50
*G. S. Chappell	b Garner	113	c Garner b Botham	39
G. J. Cosier	b Garner	44	c Taylor b Botham	2
K. D. Walters	c Denning b Burgess	23	b Botham	25
D. W. Hookes	b Botham	3	b Burgess	108
†R. W. Marsh	b Garner	3	b Garner	0
K. J. O'Keeffe	c Denning b Burgess	11	c Denning b Moseley	20
J. R. Thomson	b Burgess	0	c Botham b Garner	0
M. F. Malone	b Burgess	2	c Richards b Breakwell	17
G. Dymock	not out	0	not out	6
	Extras: 10b, 2w, 6nb	18	Extras: 15lb, 1w, 4nb	20
	Total ..	232	Total ..	289

Fall of wickets: 1-2, 2-57, 3-177, 4-197, 5-200, 6-204, 7-223, 8-223, 9-231

1-16, 2-18, 3-141, 4-172, 5-183, 6-214, 7-251, 8-252, 9-271

Bowling

	O	M	R	W	O	M	R	W
Garner	20	8	66	4	23	6	71	2
Moseley	16	5	52	0	17	6	55	1
Burgess	9.3	2	25	5	9	3	41	1
Botham	15	2	48	1	22	6	98	4
Breakwell	7	0	23	0	0.3	0	4	1

Somerset

B. C. Rose	not out	110	c Marsh b Thomson	27
P. W. Denning	c Marsh b Dymock	39	b Chappell	34
I. V. A. Richards	c Hookes b Malone	18	c Cosier b O'Keeffe	53
*D. B. Close	c McCosker b Malone	0		
D. Breakwell	c Chappell b O'Keeffe	23		
I. T. Botham	c McCosker b O'Keeffe	59	not out	39
P. A. Slocombe	not out	55	not out	8
†D. J. S. Taylor				
G. I. Burgess				
J. Garner				
H. R. Moseley				
	Extras: 4b, 6lb, 26nb	36	Extras: 4b, 3lb, 3w, 11nb	21
	Total for 5 wkts. dec.	340	Total for 3 wkts.	182

Fall of wickets: 1-81, 2-116, 3-117, 4-146, 5-228

1-50, 2-129, 3-129

Bowling

	O	M	R	W	O	M	R	W
Thomson	16	2	60	0	12	1	57	1
Dymock	17	7	48	1	5	0	25	0
Malone	22	4	70	2	9	2	18	0
O'Keeffe	35	15	114	2	5.1	0	32	1
Chappell	2	0	11	0	8	4	29	1
Walters	2	1	1	0				

* Captain   † Wicketkeeper   Umpires: H. D. Bird, T. W. Spencer

A talented quartet – from left to right:
Vic Marks, Ian Botham, Peter Roebuck,
Phil Slocombe. The first three players all
captained Somerset. Slocombe, a stylish
batsman, never fully realised his promise and
ended his career before he was thirty.

Hallam Moseley, born in Barbados, played for
Somerset from 1971 until 1982. He was always
popular with the fans, not only for his pace
bowling (547 first-class wickets) and his
efficiency in the field, but also because of his
pleasant personality.

Viv Richards will go down in the history of cricket as one of the greatest batsmen, but he was also a useful bowler. His medium-pacers and off-breaks claimed nearly 100 first-class wickets in his Somerset matches and almost 100 again in one-day competitions.

Tom Cartwright's main career and achievements (including a double century) were with Warwickshire, but his later years with Somerset in the 1970s were of great value. An outstanding medium-pace bowler, he took over 400 wickets at 18.86 for his new county and still proved a useful bat. Many thought he deserved more than his five Tests.

79

WESTERN Daily Press

LATE WEST

No. 39,247—Vol. 243   9p   BRITAIN'S FASTEST GROWING REGIONAL MORNING NEWSPAPER   MONDAY, SEPTEMBER 10, 1979

Suddenly, after 104 elusive years—

HOWZAT! IT'S A DOUBLE

Thanks, with £1,200 rings

By Trevor Green

SUPERMARKET store-man Mr Ron Clements thought the large brown hold-all he found was a bomb.

Instead it held £51,000-worth of jewellery which had been left-in Old Station car park, Yeovil, by a salesman.

Mr Clements, aged 45, of Plantagenet Close, Yeovil, and car park superintendent Mr Raymond Male, of Monksdale, Yeovil, took their breathtaking find to the police.

Now they have had their honesty rewarded.

Their wives each received £1,200 diamond rings as a Thank You from the company which lent the bag of gems. Manufactur-

Somerset wins the crowning glory

By Western Daily Press Sports Editor Colin Price

SOMERSET County cricketers have rolled back more than a century of failure, winning two titles in one sensational week-end.

Fishing skippers caught in a swoop

By Chris Rundle

FIVE Minehead fishing boat skippers could lose their licences after being caught fishing outside their limits.

They were netted in a carefully organised swoop involving the Board of Trade, Coastguards and West Somerset district council officials on Saturday afternoon.

They boarded a police launch brought from Avonmouth, and found the five fishing between Porlock and Lynmouth, well outside the six-mile limit from Minehead harbour placed on their operations by the council.

Fishermen in nearby Porlock had complained to the

THE ARMY MAY FUEL SECRET PLANES

By David Humphrey

TROOPS may be called in to replace civilians who normally refuel warplanes at the Boscombe Down top secret experimental base, near Salisbury.

If that happens, union officials are threatening to call on tanker drivers not to deliver fuel supplies to the base.

Boscombe, one of Britain's most sensitive military airfields, is one of several expected to be hit by stoppages by industrial civil servants today.

The base, which employs nearly 1,000 industrial civil servants, is particularly vulnerable, because its aircraft are refuelled exclusively by

Two-day strikes are on again

Front page news – a double triumph for Somerset.

Brian Rose and his men who won the Gillette Cup and the John Player League in 1979.

Rose starts the celebrations with a bottle of champagne.

The victory bus, ready for its tour of Taunton after the double victories of 1979.

Gillette Cup Final

NORTHAMPTONSHIRE v. SOMERSET

at Lord's Ground, Saturday, September 8th, 1979

Northamptonshire won the toss and elected to field

Somerset won by 45 runs

NORTHAMPTONSHIRE

1 G. Cook	run out	44
2 W. Larkins	l b w b Garner	0
3 R. G. Williams	hit wicket b Garner	8
4 A. J. Lamb	st Taylor b Richards	78
5 P. Willey	c Taylor b Garner	5
6 T. J. Yardley	c Richards b Burgess	20
*7 G. Sharp	b Garner	22
8 Sarfraz Nawaz	not out	16
9 T. M. Lamb	b Garner	4
10 B. J. Griffiths	b Garner	0
‡11 P. J. Watts	Absent Hurt	
	B 6, l-b 9, w 5, n-b 7,	27
	Total...	224

FALL OF THE WICKETS

1..3 2..13 3..126 4...138 5...170 6..186 7..218 8...224 9..224 10...

Bowling Analysis	O	M	R	W	Wd.	N-b
Garner	10.3	3	29	6	...	5
Botham	10	3	27	0	5	...
Jennings	12	1	29	0	...	...
Burgess	9	1	37	1	...	2
Marks	4	0	22	0	...	...
Richards	9	0	44	1	...	...
Breakwell	2	0	9	0	...	...

SOMERSET

‡1 B. C. Rose	b Watts	41
2 P. W. Denning	c Sharp b Sarfraz	19
3 I. V. A. Richards	b Griffiths	117
4 P. M. Roebuck	b Willey	14
5 I. T. Botham	b T. Lamb	27
6 V. J. Marks	b Griffiths	9
7 G. I. Burgess	c Sharp b Watts	1
8 D. Breakwell	b T. Lamb	5
9 J. Garner	not out	24
*10 D. J. S. Taylor	not out	1
11 K. F. Jennings		
	B 5, l-b 3, w , n-b 3,	11
	Total...	269

FALL OF THE WICKETS

1...34 2...95 3...145 4...186 5...213 6...214 7...219 8...268 9... 10...

Bowling Analysis	O	M	R	W	Wd.	N-b
Sarfraz	12	3	51	1	...	2
Griffiths	12	1	58	2	...	...
Watts	12	2	34	2	...	1
T. Lamb	12	0	70	2	...	...
Willey	12	2	45	1	...	...

‡Captain

Umpires—D. J. Constant & J. G. Langridge

* Wicket-keeper

Scorers—J. Mercer, E. Brice & E. Solomon

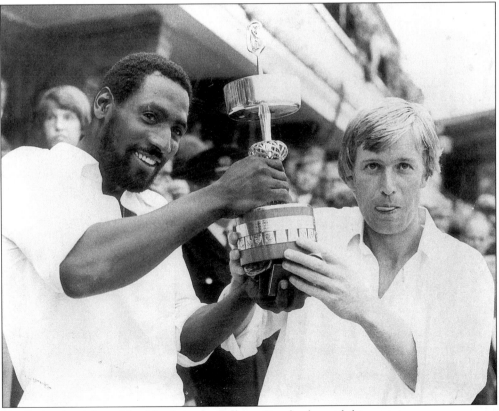

Viv Richards – Man of the Match in the Gillette Cup final – with his captain.

Somerset's cricketers in that memorable summer of 1979. From left to right, back row: V.J. Marks, P.M. Roebuck, C.H. Dredge, J. Garner, D. Gurr, H. Moseley, K.F. Jennings, T. Gard. Front row: D. Breakwell, M.J. Kitchen, P.W. Denning, B.C. Rose, D.J.S. Taylor, I.V.A. Richards, I.T. Botham.

The loyal fans who cheered them on to their early cup triumphs.

Man of the Match Vic Marks with
Brian Rose and another trophy for
Somerset. Nottinghamshire were
dismissed for 130 and beaten
by 9 wickets in the 1982 Benson and
Hedges final at Lord's. Marks conceded
only 24 runs in his 11 overs and
claimed two crucial wickets: those of
Derek Randall and the captain, Clive
Rice, who were both bowled.

Vic Marks, a farmer's son from Middle
Chinnock, took 738 first-class wickets
and over 200 in one-day competitions
for Somerset with his off-spin. His
career best was 8 for 17 against
Lancashire at Bath. A genuine
all-rounder, he hit nearly 10,000 runs,
including four centuries. Marks played
in six Tests and 34 one-day
internationals. He left the game after
fifteen seasons with Somerset for a new
career as a journalist, having captained
the county in his last two seasons.

Another world-class player from overseas who played for Somerset was Sunil Gavaskar, seen here with his opening partner, Brian Rose. The prodigious Indian had just one season with the county, but provided some rewarding cricket for the crowds.

Then there was New Zealand's Martin Crowe, another master batsman, who first came to Somerset as an unknown twenty-one-year-old. He averaged nearly 60 in his 48 county matches, including a double century and 13 other first-class centuries.

Celebrating a Somerset cup triumph is Graham Burgess, one of the county's popular stalwarts who, while never in the reckoning for a Test place, gave years of yeoman service to the club. 'Budgie', who was born in Glastonbury, scored over 7,000 runs and took nearly 500 wickets in first-class matches with his medium-pacers.

One of Somerset's best wicketkeepers, Derek Taylor, emigrated with his wife to Australia after the 1982 season. He received farewell gifts from the club chairman, Max Jeffrey (left), and the supporters' chairman, Ken Wills. Taylor claimed 661 dismissals in his 280 first-class games and, in the Benson and Hedges competition, set a record of eight catches in a one-day match. He scored nearly 7,000 first-class runs and opened the batting when needed.

All-round action from Somerset's greatest cricketer, Ian Botham, captured by the artist David Stribbling in this picture in the museum.

Ian Botham's incredible achievements with bat and ball have been recorded in many books. His legendary performances for England overshadow those for Somerset, but there is plenty to remember from his matches for the county he grew up in – including an unforgettable 228 off Gloucestershire at Taunton in 1980 when he was twenty-four. In 1985, he beat Arthur Wellard's record of 66 sixes in a season with 80 in first-class matches plus 20 in one-day competitions. Botham averaged 36.04 for Somerset in first-class games and took 489 wickets at 26.52.

Somerset's highest individual innings: 322 by Viv Richards against Warwickshire at Taunton in 1985.

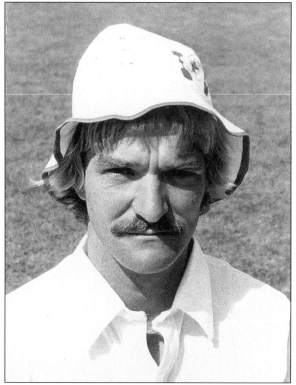

Colin Dredge, the 'Demon from Frome', flanked by Viv Richards and Joel Garner. Dredge is another in the ranks of those who have given unstinting service to their native county on the cricket field. He took nearly 450 wickets with his medium-fast deliveries in first-class games and over 250 in one-day appearances.

Peter Denning, born at Chewton Mendip, was another wholehearted player. He was a left-handed batsman, popularly known as 'Dasher' for his scampered singles. He shared Somerset's record fourth-wicket stand of 310 in 1980 with Ian Botham. He was out for 98 on that occasion, but scored eight centuries in his 11,559 first-class runs, with an average of nearly 30. In one-day matches, he won seven Man of the Match awards.

Making his debut in the Second XI at thirteen, Peter Roebuck went on to become one of the most dependable batsman Somerset has ever had. Only three players have scored more first-class runs for the county than his 16,212 (av. 38.34), and his 31 centuries included an unbeaten double century. Many fans have no doubt he should have opened for England. He captained Somerset from 1986 until 1988 and later led Devon. Like Vic Marks, he has made a name for himself with his journalism and books.

A chirpy character with an infectious enthusiasm, Dennis Breakwell joined Somerset from Northamptonshire (and shared a flat in Taunton with Viv Richards and Ian Botham). He took 281 first-class wickets with his slow left-arm deliveries and his only century (against New Zealand in 1978) is treasured by his fans. After his playing days, Dennis coached youngsters at the county ground and is now coach at King's College, Taunton.

Shepton Mallet on Saturday 8 November 1986 was a traumatic occasion for Somerset. At the end of the season, the committee had decided to part with their West Indian stars, Viv Richards and Joel Garner, and bring back Martin Crowe as their overseas player. Ian Botham had made it clear that if the West Indian duo went, he would go too. The ensuing uproar among members culminated at a special meeting when a motion of no confidence in the committee was debated. Members came from far afield, many arriving long before the start. The 'rebels' lost the day, the motion failing by 1,828 votes to 798, and Richards, Garner, and Botham played no more for Somerset. The latter moved first to Worcestershire and later to Durham. The wounds healed slowly, and after seven years the three accepted life membership of Somerset and in 1998 Botham opened the members' new stand named after him.

A last goodbye for Viv and Joel

*Daily Mail
10.11.86*

Nigel Popplewell

It was delivered by Cambridge Blue Nigel Popplewell

By PETER JACKSON

THE SOMERSET rebels knew they were stumped the moment Nigel Popplewell stood up before a crowd of 3,000 and revealed what life was like in a dressing room with three superstars.

During a courageous two minutes in the 'witness box' the county's former opening batsman demolished an 11-week campaign for the reinstatement of Viv Richards and Joel Garner with an attack that ensured a 70 per cent. confirmation of their sacking.

'Popplewell's speech was the killer,' said one of the rebel leaders before all the votes had been counted. 'Until then we thought we were in with a fighting chance. There was no pulling it round after that.'

The Shepton Mallet meeting and its outcome were the big sports story of the day in countless newspapers.

The captain, Peter Roebuck, and chairman of the club, Michael Hill, listen intently to the debate at the big meeting.

93

One from Sydney, the other from Barbados – two great batsmen together at Taunton. Steve Waugh averaged 78.76 in his two summers as Somerset's overseas player, with eight centuries in his 19 first-class games and he headed the national averages in his second season at the club (1988). Roy Marshall, who played for Hampshire and was one of the most exciting batsman of the 1950s and 1960s, went to Taunton to coach at King's College and served as Somerset's cricket chairman for several years.

Cambridge Blue Nigel Popplewell joined Somerset as an all-rounder and made his mark mainly as a batsman. His 143 in 62 minutes off Gloucestershire at Bath in 1983 included Somerset's fastest-ever century (41 minutes) – a remarkable innings, even if it included a certain amount of friendly bowling in quest of a declaration. The best of his four centuries was his 172 off Essex at Southern two years later, when he and Roebuck put on 243 for the first wicket. Popplewell left Somerset when he was twenty-eight, to become a solicitor.

Statistics can mislead, but hardly in the case of Jimmy Cook, the hitherto little-known opening batsman from South Africa, who was thirty-six when he arrived in Taunton in 1989. By the time he had left in 1991, he had scored 7,606 first-class runs for Somerset at an average of 72.41.

Jimmy Cook receiving a presentation from Somerset's cricket manager, Jack Birkenshaw. Cook's 28 centuries included 313 not out at Cardiff, and two unbeaten double centuries.

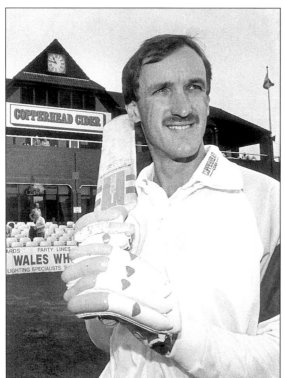

With 31 Tests to his credit, Chris Tavare came to Somerset from Kent in 1989 and, the following year, succeeded Vic Marks as captain for four seasons. A fluent stroke-maker who could keep the score moving without rashness, he averaged 43, with 6,365 runs in his 102 first-class games for Somerset – including a double century in 1990. Chris also contributed many invaluable innings in one-day competitions.

A quartet of talent in these new signings of 1987. From left to right: Neil Mallender (from Northamptonshire), who was called up to bowl for England twice in his seven years with Somerset; Graham Rose (Middlesex), who proved to be a top all-rounder; Adrian Jones (Sussex), a bowler with real pace; Neil Burns (Essex), a wicketkeeper who could also score runs.

Five
The County Ground

It was the original intention of the founders of Somerset CCC not to have a county ground, but within a few years the club had taken up residence at the present ground (within a six hit or two of the centre of Taunton). Of over 1,200 first-class matches Somerset have played at home, more than 700 have been here, as well as the great majority of one-day matches.

Almost 250 first-class fixtures have been at Bath, nearly 200 at Weston-super-Mare and the rest shared between no fewer than ten other grounds around the county, mainly Frome, Glastonbury, Wells and Yeovil. In the one-day competitions, Somerset have even ventured outside the county to Torquay.

Apart from a week in Bath, Taunton is now the club's only home venue, and the many improvements and new facilities provided in the last quarter of a century – the most recent being the Ian Botham stand and the indoor school complex – have made it one of the best of all the smaller first-class grounds anywhere.

This unfinished sketch of the county ground at Taunton, seen from across the River Tone, probably dates from 1882, the year the grandstand was built. Penny-farthing bicycles can be seen on the track round the ground.

A century ago there was little provision of any kind for the public, other than wooden benches.

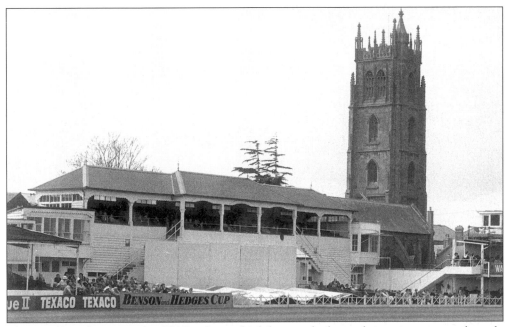

The stand now known as the Old Pavilion, which has much changed since it was erected nearly 120 years ago. Between the pavilion and St James' church is the churchyard, to which many balls have been dispatched.

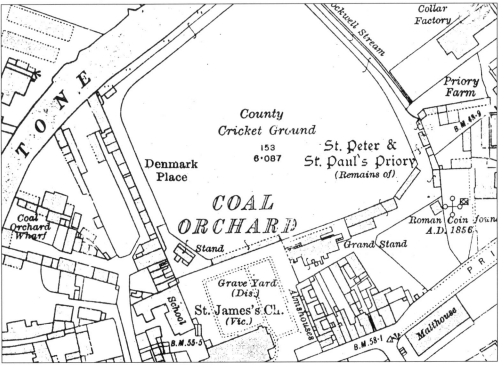

This 1914 map shows how little there was in the way of structures worthy of being recorded on the ground (a situation that remained for many years to come). At one time, women in the cottages bordering the west edge of the ground sold refreshments to spectators.

'Is Wellard batting?' – three youngsters, named on this picture of around 1932 as Jack Ewens, Ray Skinner, and Ron North, get a free look at the match.

A view of the ground from where the Colin Atkinson pavilion now stands.

An aerial view of the ground before the major developments which have taken place in the last twenty years – including the Colin Atkinson pavilion, the indoor school complex, and the Ian Botham stand.

The J.C. White gates were erected in 1963 at the St James' Street entrance, in memory of one of Somerset's greatest cricketers. Three of the county's best-known players of the 1950s and 1960s look on, from left to right: Brian Langford, Harold Stephenson, and Bill Alley.

'Farmer' White's widow receives a bouquet at the opening ceremony.

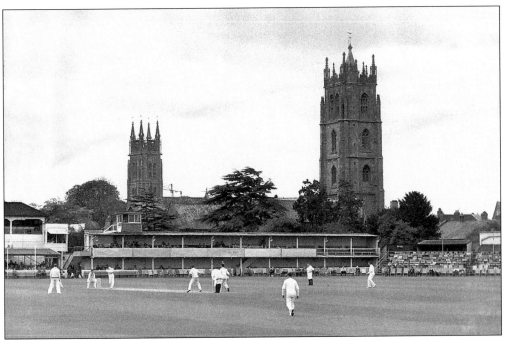

The Ridley Stand was erected between the Old Pavilion and the Stragglers' Pavilion in 1926. It was provided by the club's then president, Col. H.M. Ridley.

Greyhound racing was staged at the county ground for some time after the Second World War.

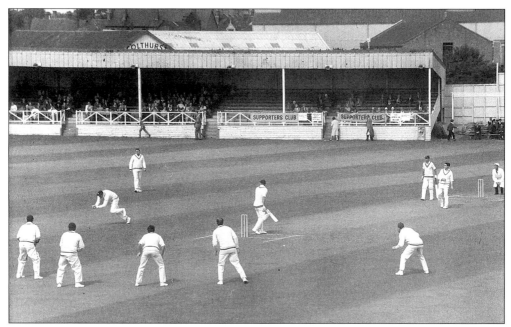

The River Stand was provided by the supporters' club, which was formed in 1953 to give much-needed financial and other help for the cricket club. The supporters raised many thousands of pounds, mainly by a football competition. Yorkshire are fielding in this picture and Fred Trueman has just bowled.

The opening ceremony for the River Stand. From left to right: Air Vice-Marshal M.L. Taylor (*club secretary*), A.H. Southwood (*chairman*), the Bishop of Bath and Wells, Dr. H.W. Bradfield (*president*), and Rex Frost (*president of the supporters' club*).

The new pavilion, later to be named the Colin Atkinson Pavilion.

The opening ceremony was performed, during the Australians' visit in 1981, by Peter May, the president of MCC. From left to right: Michael Hill (*vice-chairman*), Max Jeffrey (*chairman*), Colin Atkinson (*president*), David Seward (*secretary*), Peter May, and the Mayor and Mayoress of Taunton.

A view of the north side of the ground before developments in recent years.

The cricket shop at the county ground has had various homes, including this double-decker bus.

The first floodlit cricket match on any county ground was staged at Taunton in September 1982, when the West Indies beat Somerset by 17 runs.

The pavilion on the same occasion. Over 6,500 people were at the challenge match.

A scene that has vanished only in recent times: the outdoor nets have gone to enable more car-parking space to be provided at the St James' Street entrance.

A familiar face for many years around the ground: Charlie Sedgebeer, the scorecard seller, was presented with an illuminated address on his retirement in 1963.

Head groundsman Phil Frost (with broom) won the national Groundsman of the Year title three times in the mid-1990s.

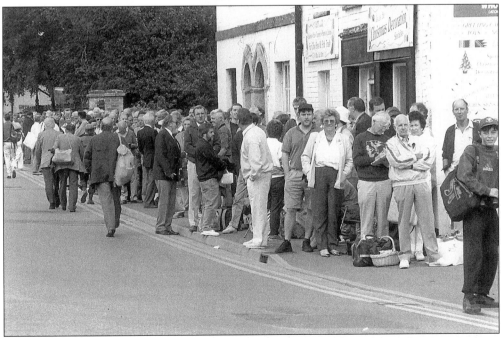

A long queue for one of Somerset's big home ties stretches from the St James' Street entrance to the church.

Cecil Buttle (right), Somerset's head groundsman for many years, deep in discussion with Bert Lock during a visit by the latter in the late 1960s. Lock, after his long career as Oval groundsman, was the Test and County Cricket Board's official inspector of pitches.

Two more familiar faces at the county ground: Tom Tout (left), a member of the office staff and for many years the club's scorer, and Nobby Clark, steward.

Six
Miscellany

On the edge of the county ground is one of Taunton's historic buildings, the Priory Barn, scheduled for many years as an ancient monument. In fact it was probably a rest house for visitors to the fifteenth-century priory, of which it is the only remaining structure. Only in more recent times was it used as a barn and, later, a builder's store.

The dilapidated building was acquired by the Supporters' Club and, after years of hard work by a small band of enthusiasts (including the raising of £100,000), opened in 1989 as Somerset Cricket Museum. It houses a fascinating and very varied collection of cricket memorabilia, mainly linked to Somerset, and attracts many visitors. There are also large reference and lending libraries.

This last section includes a miscellany of more photographs from the hundreds in the museum's archives.

The Priory Barn in the 1950s, when it was used as a builder's store. (Crown Copyright picture)

The building as it is today, a cricket museum with reference and lending libraries on the upper floor. The benches outside were part of the seating at the Nursery End at Lord's for over fifty years.

The museum's patron, Lord Archer of Weston-super-Mare, at the 'pavilion end' of the museum.

The museum was the brainchild of the late Rex Frost, Somerset's treasurer and president of the Supporters' Club for many years. He is pictured here at the Victorian printing press, which was used to produce scorecards for a long time. The printer's aim was to add the fall of a wicket before the departing batsman could reach the pavilion.

A bat-making demonstration in the museum by Julian Millichamp, of well-known bat-making firm Millichamp and Hall, whose premises are near the museum.

The bat with which Ian Botham scored one of the greatest of all Test centuries is handed over to museum curator Tony Stedall by Plymouth schoolboy Tom Higgins. After Botham's match-winning 149 not out off the Australians at Headingley in 1981, the bat passed through various hands. At one time, Tom used it for playing cricket in his garden, before it was decided that the museum was the right place for the bat.

Five men with a lot of cricket to remember: David Mills (seated), the editor of *Memories of Somerset Cricket*, with, from left to right: Bill Alley, Brian Rose, Eric Hill, and Bryan Lobb.

It's over and we've won! A pitch invasion at the county ground.

TAUNTON'S BIG DAY

By Eric Coombes

INTERNATIONAL cricket came to Taunton for the first time last summer, with England meeting Sri Lanka in a Prudential World Group A match on Saturday, June 11th, 1983.

Only a week after the square had been awash in a violent thunderstorm which wiped out Somerset's John Player League match against Essex, head groundsman Gordon Prossor had produced a peach of a wicket for the big day.

And the large crowd, who had begun queuing outside the gates in the early hours of the morning, were rewarded with some sparkling batting as England rattled up 333-9 in their 60 overs.

David Gower struck five sixes in a superb 130, Allan Lamb produced some magnificent strokes in his 53 and Ian Gould and Graham Dilley plundered 35 and 29 respectively towards the end.

The great disappointment was that Somerset hero Ian Botham was run out without scoring, but Vic Marks restored West Country pride with 5-39 off his 12 overs as the determined Sri Lankans were eventually bowled out for 286 in 58 overs.

And Botham, never to be kept out of the action for long, held a stunning slip catch off Dilley to dismiss the Sri Lanka skipper, Dias for two.

ENGLAND

G. Fowler b John	22
C.J. Tavaré c de Alwis b Ranatunge	32
D.I. Gower b de Mel	130
A.J. Lamb b Ratnayake	53
M.W. Gatting run out	7
I.T. Botham run out	0
§I.J. Gould c Ranatunge b Ratnayake	35
G.R. Dilley b de Mel	29
V.J. Marks run out	5
P.J.W. Allott not out	0
*R.G.D. Willis	
Extras (lb 11, w 8, nb 1)	20
Total (for 9, 60 overs)	333

Fall of wickets:
49, 78, 174, 193, 194, 292, 298, 333, 333

Bowling: de Mel 12-3-62-2; John 12-0-55-1 Ratnayake 12-0-66-2; Ranatunge 12-0-65-1 de Silver 12-0-65-0

SRI LANKA

S. Wettimuny lbw b Marks	33
B. Kuruppu c Gatting b Dilley	4
R. Dias c Botham b Dilley	2
*R.L.D. Mendis c Willis b Marks	56
R.S. Madugalle c Tavaré b Marks	12
A. Ranayunge c Lamb b Marks	34
D.S. Silva st Gould b Marks	28
§R.G. de Alwis not out	58
A.L.F. de Mel c Dilley b Allott	27
R.J. Ratnayake c Lamb b Dilley	15
V.B. John b Dilley	0
Extras (lb 12, w 2, nb 3)	17
Total (58 overs)	286

Fall of wickets:
11, 17, 92, 108, 117, 168, 192, 246, 281

Bowling: Willis 11-3-43-0; Dilley 11-0-45-4 Allott 12-1-82-1; Botham 12-0-60-0; Marks 12-3-39-5

Umpires: M.J. Kitchen & K.E. Palmer   *Captian; §Wicketkeeper

England won by 47 runs   Man-of-the-Match: David Gower

The first World Cup game at Taunton. Memories of the England v. Sri Lanka encounter in 1983, published in the club's yearbook.

Somerset surpasses almost every other county in the number of umpires it has produced in recent times. Here are eight together, from left to right, back row: Peter Eele, Roy Palmer, John Harris, Mervyn Kitchen. Front row: Peter Wight, Ken Palmer, Bill Alley, Alan Whitehead.

Bill Alley and Ken Palmer take the field. Both became Test umpires.

Morlands Athletic Ground, Glastonbury, where Somerset played eighteen first-class matches between 1952 and 1973.

The pavilion at Glastonbury is declared open by Somerset's captain, Maurice Tremlett, during the Somerset *v.* Middlesex match held there in 1956. Bill Edrich (in front of the glass door) and Denis Compton (behind Tremlett) were among those present.

'Mr Wells from Assam', roughly dressed and smoking a pipe, was among those in the Somerset Stragglers' team at Curry Rivel on August Bank Holiday 1925. His real identity was Bill Greswell, the Somerset bowler who was one of the first and best exponents of in-swing. Due to the First World War and his work as a tea-planter in Ceylon, he played only 115 matches for Somerset, but took over 450 wickets and is regarded as one of Ceylon's greatest European players. He was Somerset's president from 1962 until 1965.

The ranks of Somerset's many amateur players a century ago included several professional soldiers, but just one future admiral – Cecil Spenser Hickley. His cricket career was less distinguished than his naval one, however. He played five matches in 1898 and 1899, when in his mid-thirties, and scored a total of 82 runs.

Somerset takes its message to the skies during a Sunday League match in 1980.

A big membership campaign launched in Wells in 1962 is discussed by patron-in-chief Lord Hylton (left) and the club chairman, 'Bunty' Longrigg.

Six from Somerset in one Test match, including both captains! Answering a photo-call before England *v*. West Indies at Headingly in 1980 are Viv Richards, Brian Rose, Joel Garner, and Ian Botham, flanked by umpires and former Somerset players Ken Palmer and Bill Alley. Botham and Richards were the captains.

A busy Botham cuts down travelling time and lands at the county ground by helicopter.

Adrian Jones (right), Somerset fast bowler, is congratulated by team-mate Graham Rose on another wicket. Jones' career-best figures were 7 for 30 against Hampshire at Southampton in 1988.

The Dutch connection began in 1990, when all-rounder Roland Lefebvre made his debut for Somerset. His tight medium-pacers could be hard to score off, and he once hit a century. After three seasons, he joined Glamorgan. His fellow countryman, Andre van Troust, 6ft 7in tall and capable of very fast deliveries, made his debut in 1991 and is still playing for the county.

Somerset can boast one of the most loyal followings of any of the first-class counties.

Apart from his years as a player, Bill Andrews is well remembered as a valued coach and a discoverer of talent.

A picture of the legendary Sammy Woods is received on behalf of the club by Michael Hill (left) and Tony Brown (right) – Somerset's then chairman and secretary respectively – from Hugh Bradford and Dick Morrish, both life vice-presidents.

Bahamas-bound for some warm-up matches, Somerset players prepare to set off from the county ground. From left to right: Ian Swallow, Andy Hayhurst, Vic Marks, and Chris Tavare. The last three players have all captained the county.

Few have served Somerset for so long in different capacities as Peter Robinson (right), being presented here with a clock by chief executive Peter Anderson in 1990 to mark twenty-five years with the club. Robinson joined the county in 1965 as an all-rounder and became coach when his playing days with the First XI ended in 1977. He has also been the Second XI supremo and, more recently, was appointed director of youth cricket.

There are few who can have spent more time at the county ground than Eric Hill, who was coached there as a boy before the Second World War. After service in the RAF (hazardous reconnaissance flights deep into enemy territory earned him two decorations), he opened the batting for Somerset, with Harold Gimblett, from 1947 until 1951. Hill later captained the Second XI. Then, for over forty years, until he retired in 1998, he was a respected cricket journalist, always to be seen in his seat in the press box.

Ian Botham on one of his long-distance charity walks.

Botham raised nearly £900,000 for leukaemia research in 1986.

The club's chief executive, Peter Anderson, walked the boundaries of the county to raise money for Somerset cricket. Fellow walkers were the late Eric Coombes (right), a sports journalist, and Jim Hayle, of Britannic Assurance.

While in the Second XI in 1991, Andy Caddick, Somerset's New Zealand-born pace bowler, took 96 wickets in 15 matches, to win a Rapid Cricket Line Player of the Year award. Also pictured are Rapid Cricket Line's representative (left) and coach Peter Robbinson. Caddick was in England's Test team two years later and, in 1998, he topped 100 first-class wickets in a season.

Joel Garner and a fan.